LECTURES AND ESSAYS.

BY

HENRY GILES.

IN TWO VOLUMES.

VOLUME I.

BOSTON:
TICKNOR, REED, AND FIELDS.
MDCCCLI.

CAMBRIDGE:
PRINTED BY BOLLES AND HOUGHTON.

Third Thousand.

PREFACE.

The greater part of the following pages consists of oral addresses, delivered in mixed and popular assemblies. The author in giving them to the press, acts upon a desire expressed in various directions to see them in this form; and if they shall be read with a portion of the kindness with which they were heard, the author will be content. He is clearly aware, that they have, in full measure, the faults that mark the class of compositions to which they belong, but he trusts that they are not wholly wanting in some of the characteristic merits of such compositions. The author does not presume to attribute any permanent or critical value to these pages; yet to the author, personally, they have a greater value, though of another kind; they call up hours passed in living communion with his audiences; memories of generous sympathies, of hospitable bounties, of friendly encouragements, of general regard, which he would scarcely exchange for the proudest merely literary reputation.

The other pieces, as will be seen, were contributed to periodicals. The principal of them were furnished to a religious journal, and are accordingly of a subdued and serious tone.

The circumstances of the author left him but few opportunities for sustained, close, consecutive study. But though compelled to write casually and hastily, he has always endeavored to write truthfully and thoughtfully.

BOSTON, JANUARY, 1850.

CONTENTS.

LECTURES AND ESSAYS.

FALSTAFF.

A TYPE OF EPICUREAN LIFE.

Our purpose in the present Essay is to make some remarks on the character of Falstaff, and on that phase of human life which the character presents and illustrates.

When George the Fourth was Prince of Wales, every body knows that he had a dandy companion called Beau Brummell, and every body also knows, that for some liberty taken with his royalty, the prince discarded the dandy. The anecdote is equally familiar, that one day Brummell and a nobleman of his acquaintance came casually in contact with the prince, when the prince courteously noticed the lord, and studiously slighted the beau. The beau, with the most imperturbable indifference, while his highness was yet in hearing, said to the lord, "Pray who is that *fat* friend of yours?" We have here to speak of one, who was not indeed a fat Prince of Wales, but a very *fat* friend to a very *lean* Prince of Wales: indeed a fat man is almost synonymous with a fat friend. There is something cordial in a fat man. Every body likes him, and he likes every body. Your Ishmaelites are, in truth, a bareboned race; a lank tribe they are, — all skeleton and bile. Food does a fat man good; it clings to him; it fructifies upon him; he swells nobly out, and fills a generous space in life. He is a living, walking-minister of gratitude to the bounty of the earth and the fullness thereof; an incarnate testimony against the vanities of care; a radiant manifestation of the wisdom of good humor. A fat man, therefore, almost in virtue of being a fat man, is, *per se*, a popular man; and commonly he deserves his popularity. In a crowded vehicle the fattest man will ever be the most ready to make room. Indeed, he seems half sorry for his size, lest it be in the way of others; but others would not have him less than he is; for his humanity is usually commensurate with his bulk. A fat man has abundance of rich juices. The hinges of his system are well oiled; the springs of his being are noiseless; and so he goes on his way rojoicing, in full contentment and placidity. It is not thus with your thin people ; the disease of leanness has manifold discomforts. Their joints are dry ; they creak like rusty axles, and from the want of due moisture, their tempers become as sharp as their bones. A fat man feels his position solid in the world ; he knows that his being is *cognisable;* he knows that he has a marked place in the universe, and that he need take no extraordinary pains to advertise mankind that he is among them ; he knows that he is in no danger of being overlooked. Your thin man is uncertain, and therefore he is uneasy. He may vanish any hour into nothing ; already he is almost a shadow, and hence it is that he uses such laborious efforts to convince you of his existence ; to persuade you that he is actually something ; that he is more than non-entity ; that he is a positive substance as well as his corpulent fellow-creature. To make this the more apparent, he tries with all his might to compensate the weakness of his step by the rapidity of his motions, and the feebleness of his voice by the solemn dignity of his utterance. But what a vain task is his ! The fat man has only to appear, and the creature is absolutely lost in the ample obscurity of the fat man's shadow ; the fat man has only to speak, and he drowns the treble squeal of his fleshless brother, in the depths of his bass, as the full swell of an organ overpowers the whistle of a penny trumpet. The fat man has only to move, and it is as the tread of an elephant beside the skip of a grasshopper. It really does take a deal of wrong to make one actually hate a fat man; and, if we are not always so cordial to a thin man as we ought to be, Christian charity should take into account the force of prejudice which we have to overcome against his *thinness.* A fat man is the nearest to that most perfect of figures, a mathematical sphere; a thin man to that most limited of conceivable dimensions, a simple line. A fat man is a being of harmonious volume, and holds relations to the material universe in every direction; a thin man has nothing but length; a thin man, in fact, is but the *continuation of a point.* Well, then, might Falstaff exult in his size; well might he mock at the prince, and his other lean cotemporaries; and accordingly, when he would address the prince in terms the most degrading, he heaps epithet upon epithet, each expressive of the utmost leanness; "Away, you starveling," he exclaims; "you elf-skin; you dried neat's tongue, you stock fish: O, for breath to utter what is like thee!"

The gross idea of Falstaff is that of a coward, a liar, a glutton and a buffoon. This idea is so partial, that when taken for the whole character it is untrue. Much more than this there must be, in one among the greatest of Shakspeare's creations. In the cowardice of Falstaff there is much inconsistency; and much of this, we may suppose, arises from the exaggerations in which the poet has knowingly indulged for the sake of ludicrous position. I do not know otherwise how to interpret the affair at Gad's Hill. The prince, whether as Shakspeare or history represents him, was no lover of dastards; yet the poet allows him to intrust Falstaff with a company; and Falstaff himself, as he gives him to us after the battle of Shrewsbury, says, "I have led my raggamuffins where they are peppered; there 's but three of my hundred and fifty left alive." Falstaff willingly goes twice to the wars; and the cool mockery of which he was capable on the field, shows a light heart, and not a timid one. The gayety, the ease, the merriment, the reckless frolic, the immovable self-possession which he exhibits, preceding the campaign and in it, evinces any other temper than that of cowardice. A coward may have daring in the midst of danger, but he has never levity in it, — spontaneous, unaffected levity. Falstaff, physically, was not a craven. He was assuredly attached to life, and to the life of the *senses.* It was all he had; it was all he hoped; and it was all he wished. He was therefore in no anxiety to lose it; and his philosophy taught him of nothing which was a compensation for endangering it.

"Hal," he says, "if thou seest me fall down in battle, and bestride me so, 't is a point of friendship."

"Nothing," says the prince, "but a colossus can do that friendship. Say thy prayers, and farewell."

"I would it were bed-time, Hal, and all well."

"Why, thou owest God a death."

"'T is not due yet, and I would be loath to pay him before his day."

This, though banter, is all congruous with his system. And, also, what can he be but joking, when he says to the prince:

"But tell me, Hal, art thou not horribly afeard? Thou being heir apparent, could the world pick thee out three such enemies again, as that fiend Douglas, that spirit Percy, and that devil Glendower? Art thou not horribly afeard? doth not thy blood thrill at it?"

No coward reveals his character in this manner, and surely this is not the way in which Shakspeare would reveal it. Falstaff gives us the truth of his character, when he says, "Indeed I am not John of Gaunt, your grandfather; but yet no coward, Hal." Falstaff was an epicure, but no glutton. He was not a great eater, for his bill contained a halfpennyworth of bread to an intolerable quantity of sack. And although Falstaff was a large drinker, he was no inebriate. And here we conceive a consummate art in Shakspeare, who sustains Falstaff throughout in our intellectual respect. He presents to our fancy a character whose life was in the senses ; whose atmosphere was the tavern, whose chief good was conviviality, and yet who never once passes the line where mind lies conquered by excess.

If the name of buffoon can be applied to Falstaff, then it is a designation not inconsistent with the richest prodigality of talents. Falstaff companioned with the highest of the land, not only on the ground of his genius, but of his rank. That Falstaff was not unmindful of his genius, appears every where in the spirit of a confident egotism, which never strikes us as puerile or foolish, and he constantly shows the same fact in direct expression. Subscribing a very characteristic letter to the prince, he shows that he was equally confident of his rank, when he writes, "Jack Falstaff, with my familiars; John, with my brothers and sisters; and *Sir John*, with the rest of Europe." Indeed there is in this signature, consciousness of fame as well as pride of station; and both are distinctive of the man. He was jealous of his position, and next to this, he was jealous of his abilities. While, upon occasions, he seems to abase himself, his self-abasement has always along with it more than an equivalent in self-elation. "Men of all sorts," he says, "take a pride to gird at me; the brain of this foolish compounded clay, man, is not able to vent any thing that tends to laughter more than *I* invent, or is invented *on* me: I am not only witty in myself, but the cause of wit in other men." It is plain, too, that he did not esteem himself meanly beside the proudest titles. When Prince John of Lancaster says to him, parting in the forest, "Fare you well, and I in my condition shall better speak of you, than you deserve:" Falstaff mutters after him, "I would you had but the wit, 't were better than your dukedom." As to lies, they were in the way of his vocation. The highest stretch of imagination could not even suspect him of veracity; and if he had any dupes, they were strangely in love with deception. His lies, too, were the lies of a professed and known wit; they were designed only for ludicrous effect, and generally were little more than comic exaggerations. In the events at Gad's Hill, and those that immediately follow them, there is an epitome of the whole character of Falstaff; but there is, at the same time, an evident design on the part of the poet, to bring out his peculiarities with grotesque extravagance; and to produce the broadest and the most comic result. The entire scene is too long to recite, and therefore I can but recall it to your thoughts by a very abbreviated sketch.

Travellers are coming to London with money. The prince, Falstaff, and their companions, lay a plot to rob them. On the way, Falstaff is cheated from his horse, and then he is all but helpless. "Eight yards of uneven ground," he says, "is three score and ten miles afoot to me; and the stony-hearted villains know it well enough." It being dark before daybreak in the morning, Prince Henry and Poins easily separate from the party. Falstaff and the rest accomplish the robbery, and sit down to count the spoils. Prince Henry and Poins then suddenly rush upon the victors, and secure the booty. When Falstaff comes afterwards empty-handed to the inn, his burlesque is so openly broad, that we cannot suppose that so great a master of art and nature as Shakspeare ever connected such enormous, such palpable blunders with so keen an intellect as Falstaff's, except for the direct purpose of broadest comedy. Falstaff, accordingly, aims at making no ingenious excuses. He sets, at once, to lie; but upon a scale so grand, that while his hearers shall see that they are lies, they shall yet be startled at their magnitude; and, with an inconsistency so bold, that it stammers at no contradiction, blushes at no detection; with oddities so wild and full of humor, that his impudence becomes magnificent, and his drollery irresistible. This is the result which he proposes to himself, to cover the ludicrousness of his position by investing it with a circle of the most enchanting absurdity; and then, from the centre of that circle, to flash around him such corruscations, such a splendor of fun, that men shall have no power to mock him in their paroxysms of laughter, and no sight to note his humiliation for the tears of mirth that bedim their eyes; this, I say, is the result which he proposes, and this result he most successfully accomplishes. As he comes into the tavern, puffing and panting, how heroically he puts forth his indignation, as he exclaims, against the prince and his fellows, "A plague of all cowards, and a vengeance, too! marry and amen! Give me a cup of sack, boy! A plague of all cowards! Give me a cup of sack, rogue! Is there no virtue extant? You rogue, there 's lime in this sack, too. There 's nothing but roguery to be found in villanous man; yet is a coward worse than a cup of sack with lime in it — a villanous coward. Go thy way, old Jack, die when thou wilt, if *manhood*, good *manhood* be not forgotten on the face of the earth, then am I a shotten herring. There live but three good men unhanged in England, and one of them is fat, and grows old. God help, the while, a bad world, I say. I wish I were a weaver, and could sing psalms, or any thing; a plague of all cowards, I say still." As he warms to his work, the banter becomes richer. "I am a rogue," he says, "if I was not at half a sword with a dozen of them two hours together.

I have 'scaped by a miracle: I am eight times thurst through the doublet; four through the hose; my buckler cut through and through; my sword hacked like a handsaw, *ecce signum.* I never dealt better since I was a man; all would not do. A plague of all cowards! let them speak! if they, if they speak more or less than truth, they are villains, and the sons of darkness." Absurdity now deepens upon absurdity. Four come on; then sixteen; then all!

PRINCE HENRY. "What, you fought with all!"

FALSTAFF. "All? I know not what you call all! But if I fought not with fifty of them, then am I a bunch of radish: if there were not two or three and fifty upon poor old Jack, then am I no two legged creature."

POINS. "Pray God, you have not murdered some of them!"

F. "Nay, that's past praying for! for I have peppered two of them: two, I am sure, I have paid: two rogues in buckram suits: I tell thee what, Hal, if I tell thee a lie, spit in my face, call me horse! Thou knowest my old ward. Here I lay, and thus I bore my point. Four rogues in buckram let drive at me."

P. H. "What! four? thou saidst two, even now."

F. "Four, Hal, I told thee, four."

POINS. "Ay, he said four."

F. "These four came all afront, and mainly thrust at me. I made no more ado, but took all their seven points on my target thus."

P. H. "Why there were but four even now."

F. "In buckram."

Poins. "Ay, four in buckram suits."

F. "Seven, by these hilts, or I am a villain else."

P. H. "Let him alone, we shall have more anon."

F. "Dost thou hear me, Hal?"

P. H. "Ay, and mark thee too, Jack."

F. "Do so, for it is worth listening to. These nine men in buckram that I told thee of—"

P. H. "Two more already!"

F. "Began to give ground: but I followed me close, came in foot and hand, and with a thought seven of the eleven I paid."

P. H. "O, monstrous, eleven buckram men grown out of two!"

We have then his account of three men in Kendal green, that let drive at his back, when it was so dark, that he could not see his hand.

P. H. "Why how could'st thou know these three men in Kendal green, when it was so dark that thou could'st not see thy hand! Come, tell us your reason. What say'st thou to this?"

Poins. "Come, your reason, Jack, your reason."

F. " What! upon compulsion? No: were I at the strappado, or all the racks in the world, I would not tell you on compulsion! Give you a reason on compulsion! If reasons were as plenty as blackberries, I would give no man a reason on compulsion."

The discovery is now opened. " Mark now," says the prince, " how plain a tale shall put you down," and relates the incidents as they occurred. But Falstaff, nothing confused, turns the joke completely against them, and avers that he knew them all the time. " Why, hear ye, my masters," he exclaims; " was it for me to kill the heir apparent? Should I turn upon the true prince? Why thou knowest I am as valiant as Hercules; but beware instinct: the lion will not touch the true prince. Instinct is a great matter. I was a coward upon instinct. I shall think the better of myself and thee during my life; I, for a valiant lion, and thou, for a true prince." I am not aware that the point of this excuse has been noticed by the critics, and yet I think it is especially worthy of remark. " The lion," he says, " will not touch the true prince; instinct is a great matter; I was a coward upon instinct." Why does Falstaff allude thus to a popular superstition, and why add an emphatic epithet to the title of his royal companion? Why say, the *true* prince? The reason is found in the history and feelings of the day. Henry the Fourth, father of the prince, dethroned Richard the Second, and many thought, foully caused his death; so that millions regarded him, not only as a usurper, but a murderer. His claim was unsound according to blood; he had no hold upon the national affection; and at this very time the real heir to the throne, upon hereditary grounds, was a closely guarded prisoner. This allusion, therefore, of Falstaff, implies not only the cunning pungency of a brilliant wit, but the adroit flattery of a polished courtier.

The character of Falstaff, as I apprehend, consists in the union of fine mental faculties with low appetites. This it will be my endeavor to elucidate.

If we were to take two separate characters from Shakspeare, the elements of which combined, and duly intermingled, should embody the totality of life, they would be, I think, the character of Hamlet and the character of Falstaff. Each of these characters stands, as I view them, on the same level of creative genius. We have in these, intensely contrasted, the two leading tendencies of life, the ideal, and the sensual. It is not often that Shakspeare dissociates these tendencies; and never so broadly and distinctly as in this instance. Hamlet has nothing of sensualism, Falstaff has nothing of idealism. In the creation of these two great impersonations, these two great inhabitants of the imagination-world, the attention of the poet seems to have been turned with an undivided force to opposite directions of our nature. In Hamlet, his thoughts communed entirely with the spiritual, the mysterious, the future, the infinite, the possible. In Falstaff, he dwelt exclusively in the material, the visible, the present, the limited, and the actual. We have, accordingly, in Hamlet, meditative dreaminess; spectral visitations; strugglings with unanswerable problems; questionings of an impenetrable silence; a seeking, with passion and with tears, for hidden things that will not reveal themselves; a faith resting firmly on eternal principles, and yet a scepticism perplexed amidst inscrutable phenomena; a will moved by immediate impulse, yet losing resolution in the conflict of imaginings, and the vagueness of speculation; a strength of conception, that makes the future as the *now*, and the possible as the *real*, and yet a feebleness of purpose that hesitates before a conjecture; a grief that wanders uncomforted among the mysteries of existence; a melancholy that pines under the shadows of thought; a tragedy that has its despair, and its catastrophe, not in the madness or torture of the passions, but in the sickness of affection, and in the bewilderings of the moral reason. In Falstaff, there is not only an absence of all this, but its contrary. In Falstaff, we have the entireness of being concentrated in the palpable. The present, and the personal, and the physical, make to him the sum of existence. What *is*, what is *mine*, what can be touched, and tasted, and felt, and heard, and seen, — this on the Falstaff side of life constitutes the universe. Here are no dreams or doubts; here are no mysteries or spectres; here are no hesitances or perplexities; here are no problems or conjectures; here is no sadness from fancy, and no malady from visions; here is no questioning of the future, and no musing on the grave. And yet, underlying the whole, there is a basis of melancholy, which any one who will go deep enough below the surface cannot fail to reach. To reach this, and show it, has been one purpose of the present Essay.

If Falstaff had not such noble mental faculties, his character would be wholly without dramatic dignity, and without moral import. But this is not the case. The genius of Falstaff, in its kind, is of preëminent superiority. Perhaps there is not another among Shakspeare's marvellous creations, which more displays the amazing resources of the author. Do not measure mental power by the excellence of its direction, but by the amount of its capacity, and that of Falstaff will be placed in the highest order. His intellect is of surprising force. It has clearness, precision, rapidity, strength, and subtlety. Falstaff towers in mental superiority above all by whom he is surrounded. He has the sustained ease of conscious nobility; and this, not alone with such creatures as Shallow and Slender, but with the proud Prince Henry and the austere chief justice. He contrives, directly or indirectly, to make all subordinate that are near him. The inferior characters are directly his instruments, and indirectly Falstaff contrives to make the prince as much an appendage to him as he is to the prince. "Hal, I pray thee, trouble me no more with vanity. I would to God thou and I knew where a commodity of good names were to be bought. Thou hast done much harm upon me, Hal; God forgive thee for it! thou art able to corrupt a saint. Before I knew thee, Hal, I knew nothing; and now, am I, if a man should speak truth, as little better than one of the wicked." How full of meaning, as well as wit, is that scene where the prince, being soon to appear before his stern father, Falstaff urges him to prepare an answer, and in which Falstaff and the prince alternately counterfeit the king. Falstaff, as the king, begins by subjecting Henry to a mock examination, which he conducts with admirable gravity. "Why, being son to me, art thou so pointed at? Shall the sun of heaven prove a micher, and eat blackberries? A question not to be asked! Shall the son of England prove a thief, and take purses? A question to be asked. There is a thing, Harry, which thou hast often heard of, and it is known to many in the land, by the name of pitch: this pitch, as ancient writers do report, doth defile. So doth the company thou keepest: for, Harry, now, I do not speak to thee in drink, but in tears; not in pleasure, but in passion; not in words only, but in woes also; and yet, there is a man whom I have often noted in thy company, but I know not his name."

P. H. "What manner of man, an' it like your majesty?"

F. "A good, portly man, i' faith, and corpulent; of a cheerful look, a pleasing eye, and a most noble carriage; and, as I think, his age some fifty, or, by 'r lady approaching to threescore; and, now, I remember me, his name is Falstaff. If that man should be lewdly given, he deceiveth me; for, Harry, I see virtue in his very looks. If, then, the tree may be known by the fruit, as the fruit by the tree, then peremptorily, I speak it, there is virtue in that Falstaff. *Him* keep; the rest banish."

P. H. "Dost thou speak like a king? You stand for me, and I'll play my father."

F. "Depose me! If thou doest it half so gravely, so majestically, hang me up by the heels for a rabbit-sucker or a poulterer's hare."

Prince Henry, taking then the place of his father, treats the character of Falstaff with an extreme degree of harshness. Falstaff, as the prince, inquires with exemplary simplicity, "Whom means your grace?"

P. H. "That villanous, abominable misleader of youth, Falstaff; that old white-bearded Satan."

Falstaff, still, as prince, makes a masterly defence, in which the wit is tinged with a shade of pathos. "My lord, the man I know: but, to say that I know more harm in him than in myself were to say more than I know. That he is old, the more the pity, his white hairs witness it. If sack and sugar be a fault, God help the wicked. If to be old and merry be a sin, many an old host that I know, is damned. If to be fat be to be hated, then Pharaoh's lean kine are to be loved. No, my good lord, banish Bardolph; banish Peto, banish Poins; but, for sweet Jack Falstaff, true Jack Falstaff, valiant Jack Falstaff, and, therefore, more valiant as he is old, Jack Falstaff— banish not him, thy Harry's company! banish plump Jack Falstaff, and banish all the world."

And what is superior to his interview with the chief justice, for humor and ability. The banter is so perfect, that even the solemn magistrate cannot resent it. There is something in this interview which renders audacity sublime, a daring which rises to the topmost majesty of impudence. The highest criminal judge in England opens by charging the sybarite with an offence that threatened his life; the sybarite closes it by asking the justice for the *loan of money.* Does civilized society know of courage which can go above this? The easy impertinence of Falstaff's first address is inimitable. "Give your lordship, good time of day. I am glad to see your lordship abroad; I heard that your lordship was sick; I hope that your lordship goes abroad by advice. Your lordship, though not clean past your youth, hath some smack of age in you, some relish of the saltness of time; and I most humbly beseech your lordship to have a reverend care of your health. For the box on the ear that the prince gave you, he gave it like a rude prince, and you took it like a sensible lord. — I have checked him for it." This is being tolerably free with one of the gravest magistrates of whom history has record; a magistrate so unflinching in his office, that he sent the heir of England to prison for disrespect hardly so great. With the prince himself, Falstaff deals as freely, and gets off as well. One of Falstaff's lowest associates speaks to him thus:

"Sirrah, what humor is the prince of?"

"A good shallow, young fellow. He would have made a good pantler; he would have clipped bread well."

"They say, Poins has a good wit."

"He! a good wit! hang him, baboon: he has wit as thick as Tewksbury mustard; there is no more conceit in him than in a mallet."

"Why does the prince love him so, then?"

"Because their *legs* are of a bigness, and he plays at quoits well; and eats conger and fennel; and drinks off candles' ends for flap-dragons; and rides the wild mare with the boys; . . . . and swears with a good grace; and wears his boot very smooth, like the sign of the leg; and breeds no bate with telling of discreet stories; and such other gambol faculties he hath, that show a weak mind and an able body, for the which the prince admits him: for the prince himself is such another; the weight of a hair will turn the scales between their avoirdupois."

The prince having listened to all this, suddenly shows himself, and reproaches his describer. Falstaff, nothing in the least abashed, coolly inquires, "Didst thou hear me?"

"Yes," replies the prince; "and you *knew* me, as you did, when you ran away by Gad's Hill: you knew I was at your back, and spoke it on purpose to try my patience."

Falstaff. "No, no, not so: I did not think thou wast within hearing."

Prince Henry. "I shall drive you to confess the wilful abuse; and then, I know how to handle you."

F. "No abuse, Hal! on my honor, no abuse."

P. H. "Not? To dispraise me, and call me — pantler, and bread-chipper, and, I know not what?"

F. "No abuse, Hal."

"No abuse?" echoes Poins.

F. "No abuse, Ned! in the world; honest Ned, none! I dispraised him before the wicked, that the wicked might not fall in love with him; in which doing, I have done the part of a careful friend and a true subject, and thy father is to give me thanks for it. No abuse, Hal; none, Ned, none; no, boys, none."

I introduce these passages, not simply for their drollery, which is exquisite, but as illustrative of that command which Falstaff always maintains over his faculties; of that intellectual coolness which nothing can disturb, and that intellectual vigor which nothing can subdue.

The imagination of Falstaff is enormous. It seems to be one into which Shakspeare poured the unlimited treasures of his own. It is as profuse in the ludicrous, as the Midsummer Night's Dream is in the beautiful. It seems as if Shakspeare, seeking a wild relaxation, formed to himself a being, in which, laying aside all kingly robes, he might yet sport in his kingly genius.

The imagination of Falstaff is prodigal as nature. It seems not capable of exhaustion. Every turn of it has fresh originality of thought and phrase. It displays such a faculty of invention, that each novelty only leads us to expect another more surprising. Ideas, to ordinary apprehension, the most dissimilar, Falstaff connects with as much facility, as if they were formed only to exist together; and illustrations the most strange, when fused in the alembic of his brain, and coined with the impression of his fancy, instantly take from it solidity, brilliancy, aptitude, and worth.

Falstaff has both wit and humor; but more of wit, I think, than humor. Between wit and humor there is an evident distinction, but to subject the distinction to minute criticism, would require more time than we can spare; and, after all, it is more easy to feel than to explain it. If I should say, Alexander Pope has great wit, Charles Dickens has great humor, all would give me their assent; but if, reversing the positions, I should say, Charles Dickens has great wit, Alexander Pope great humor, the assertion would be met by an instinctive denial. Wit implies *thought;* humor, *sensibility.* Wit deals with ideas; humor, with actions and with manners. Wit may be a thing of pure imagination; humor involves sentiment and character. Wit is an essence; humor, an incarnation. Wit and humor, however, have some elements in common. Both develop unexpected analogies; both include the principles of contrast and assimilation; both detect inward resemblances amidst external differences, and the result of both is pleasurable surprise; the surprise from wit excites admiration; the surprise from humor stimulates merriment, and produces laughter. Humor is a genial quality. Laughter is, indeed, akin to weeping; and true humor is as closely allied to pity as it is abhorrent of derision. Gayety is the play of brotherhood. We may be merry with each other, like children with their playmates; no friendships will thus be broken, and we shall be drawn together only the more strongly in our humanity by the recollection of our sports. Indeed, a species of humor adheres even to our loftiest conceptions; for the ideals of truth and goodness so mock the actual doings of mankind, that, if it were not for the sorrow and humility, as well as the incongruity, which the contrast suggests, our emotion would be a feeling of the ludicrous. *Life is therefore full of irony!*

In the wit of Falstaff there is a ceaseless spirit of mockery; but this mockery is always irresistibly comic. If humor be a quality which dwells in the same character with pathos, and which is always mingled with sensibility; if it is the offspring of a sympathizing fancy, which bathes the face in tears as often as it covers it with smiles; we cannot attribute it to Falstaff. But if we mean by the humorous, only what we mean by the comic; if indeed we speak of humor simply, in reference to the ludicrous; then we must allow to Falstaff a fund of it with which nothing in comedy can be compared. The sense of the ludicrous is an undeviating condition of his intellectual life. He perceives the ludicrous in every object, in every person, in every form of emotion and of thought, in every sentiment, in every possibility of human existence. He subjects all to it; nothing escapes him; and, as his capacity is vigorous, as his perception is acute, his mockery is as formidable as it is comprehensive. No occasion arises that he cannot turn to this purpose; no mode by which it can be attained is strange to him; his talents are most effective instruments, and his victims are ever present. Is the ludicrous to be excited by the oddest reversals of positions; by the strangest perversion of qualities; by the most foreign association of attributes; by all sorts of grotesque additions, assimilations, and analogies? Falstaff exhibits unfailing resources for each and all of these modes of the comic. His wit is as rich as his imagination; as prolific as it is felicitous. It is pungent, copious, brilliant in expression, and decisive in effect. It never falls short of its aim, and it never misses it. And this rare wit is wholly devoted to the ludicrous, unsoftened by any moral feeling, and uncurbed by any moral restraint.

By how many modes does he extract nourishment for laughter from those around him; what treasures of ludicrous imaginings he lavishes upon Bardolph and his peculiarities. Dame Quickly asks him for money; he refers her to Bardolph for payment.

"He," Falstaff asserts, "had his part of it."

"Alas!" Dame Quickly replies, "he is poor, he hath nothing."

F. "How? Poor! Look upon his face! What call you rich? Let them coin his nose, let them coin his cheeks."

Falstaff turned this face to much account. "I make as good use of it as a man doth of a death's head, or a *memento mori*. I never see thy face, but I think upon hell-fire, and Dives that lived in purple; for there he is in his robes burning. If thou wert any way given to virtue, I would swear by thy face; my oath would be by this fire. But thou art altogether given over, and wert indeed, but for the light in thy face, the son of utter darkness. When thou ran'st up Gad's Hill in the night to catch my horse, if I did not think thou hadst been an *ignis fatuus*, or a ball of wild fire, there 's no purchase in money. O, thou art a perpetual triumph, an everlasting bonfire-light. Thou hast saved me a thousand marks in links and torches, walking with thee in the night, betwixt tavern and tavern, but the sack thou hast drunk me, would have bought me lights as good cheap, at the dearest chandler's in Europe. I have maintained that salamander of yours with fire, any time these two and thirty years. Heaven reward me for it."

Contempt being a prevailing quality in the character of Falstaff, the cynical constantly enters into the comical. "There 's but a shirt and a half in all my company; and the half shirt is two napkins tacked together, like a herald's coat, without sleeves; and the shirt, to say the truth, stolen from my host at St. Albans, or the red-nosed inn-keeper at Daintry. But that 's all one; they 'll find linen enough on every hedge." The same spirit acts in his system of enlistment. He had taken bribes from such of the able-bodied as could give them, and thus he holds forth to Justice Shallow, on the poor wretches whom he substitutes: "Will you tell me, Master Shallow, how to choose a man? Care I for the thewes, the stature, the bulk, and big assemblance of a man? Give me the spirit, Master Shallow. Here 's Wart; you see what a ragged appearance it is. He shall charge and discharge you with the motion of a pewterer's hammer; come off, and on, swifter than he that gibbets-on the brewer's bucket. And this same half-faced fellow, Shadow ; give me this man ; he presents no mark to an enemy ; the foeman may with as great aim level at the edge of a penknife. O give me the spare men, and spare me the great ones." When the prince finds fault with the unhappy ragamuffins whom he has collected for soldiers, his reply is not ludicrous, but ironical. "Tut, tut!" he says, "good enough to toss; food for powder, food for powder; they 'll fill a pit as well as better; tush, man, mortal men, mortal men!" Much import is there in this apparent levity; in this there is laid bare the secret of many wars, and in this there are revealed the thoughts of many conquerors.

Falstaff delights as much to associate the ludicrous with himself as with others. It is hard to say which is most laughable, his despondency or his triumph. Pensiveness of such amazing girth must be vastly moving. "Bardolph, am I not fallen away? Do I not bate? Do I not dwindle? Why, my skin hangs about me like an old lady's loose gown; why, I am withered like an old apple-john. Well, I 'll repent, and that suddenly, while I am in some liking; I shall be out of heart presently, and then I shall have no strength to repent. Company, villanous company, hath been the ruin o' me."

But, anon, we hear the high tones of exultation, thus, to Prince John of Lancaster: "Do you think me a swallow, an arrow, a bullet? Have I, in my poor old motion, the expedition of a thought? I have speeded hitherto with the very extremest inch of possibility; I have foundered nine score and odd posts; and here, travel-tainted as I am, I have, in my pure and immaculate valor, taken Sir John Colville of the Dale, a most furious knight and valorous enemy. But what of that? He saw me, and yielded. I may justly say with the hook-nosed fellow of Rome, 'I came, I saw, I overcame.'" While Falstaff delights in this manner to trifle with himself, yet he never assumes an attitude of humiliation; he takes care scrupulously to guard his pride; he is willing to be the occasion of laughter, but not the object of it. In "The Merry Wives of Windsor," therefore, the identity of the character is lost; and I have, thence, thought it needless to include that aspect of it in the present review.

Let us consider now the moral structure of this character, in connection with its moral results.

Falstaff is an Epicurean, after the lowest interpretation of Epicurus; and such is the least evil form of character, which springs from mere intellect combined with the senses. Where moral principles and sympathy are inactive, it is well that irritable and ambitious passions should be so likewise, or a great intellect would become a great scourge. Indolence, therefore, and self-indulgence, set limits to energies which would scarcely be used aright, and the love of ease becomes a safeguard against talents which the love of power would make a curse. Falstaff is of those who value each moment by what it confers of palpable enjoyment; of those who say, Let us eat and drink, for to-morrow we die; and he acted out his philosophy consistently and completely. He is true to his creed, and his practice fulfils it to the letter. He is honest and open, too, in its profession. Beyond the boundary of the actual, Falstaff discerns no reality. Out from the region of the senses he appreciates no means of happiness. Within this boundary all being exists for him; beyond it are only emptiness and death. A spiritual order of things has no hold on his convictions; and the future, which is to survive his animal economy, has no influence on his feelings. He has therefore no *sentiment.* He laughs at it. He derides it. Chivalry is to him mere vanity; glory a worthless phantom. Daring, in his view, is hot-brained folly. Danger is always to be avoided, and never to be sought. After feigning death at Shrewsbury, he thus soliloquizes: "Counterfeit? I lie. I am no counterfeit; for he is but the counterfeit of a man, who has not the life of a man; but to counterfeit dying when a man thereby liveth, is to be no counterfeit, but the true and perfect image of life indeed. The better part of valor is discretion; in the which better part I have saved my life." His reflections upon "honor" are conceived in the same absorbing materialism: "Can honor set a leg? No. Honor hath no skill in surgery, then. What is honor? A word. What is in that word honor? Air; a trim reckoning. Who hath it? He that died o' Wednesday. Doth he feel it? No. Doth he hear it? No. Is it insensible, then? Yea, to the dead. But will it not live with the living? No. Why? Detraction will not suffer it. Therefore, I'll none of it."

Falstaff has little sympathy. He loves none, and he cares for few. He is luxuriously selfish. Constant indulgence of the passions blunts every finer sensibility, and extinguishes generosity of character. The affections are narrowed by depravity, and all that corrupts the moral nature, contracts the social. The voluptuary is by necessity selfish, and the gifted voluptuary effectively so. The voluptuary of talents is selfish by instinct, and selfish by ability; by instinct he pursues merely his own gratification, and by ability he makes others the instruments of it. Thus it is with Falstaff. All are for his use, and, except for that, he esteems them of no value. The prince is to supply his money; Dame Quickly is to provide his food; the page is for his service; and Bardolph for his jests.

Seeing that so much of the selfish and the heartless enters into this character, why is it not more odious to us? The fact is, the brilliant qualities of Falstaff render him attractive; and his vicious ones are not directly or aforethought inhuman. He is not in earnest for any thing; he has no enthusiasm; he admires nothing; he coverts merely to live jovially, and to live at ease. Companions to his wish around him, fare to his taste before him; plenty of sack, and a sea-coal fire; no disturbances from justices or duns; and he would have the best Elysium he could conceive or picture. He does not love any, neither does he hate any. If he is wanting in affection, he is also void of malice. It is from this conviction that we tolerate him; that we laugh at his jokes, and revel in the prodigality of his fancy. Did we feel in him any positive inhumanity, his jokes would disgust, and his fancy would revolt us. And, besides, selfish though he be, there is a sort of rude friendliness about him. Though he *uses* Bardolph, he does not *abuse* him. Even when he is most exacting, he pays back more than he receives, in the humor and the wit by which he diversifies the lives of those who serve him; and this he seems to know most thoroughly, and not to set it any whit below its value. He is often grotesque, but he is never tyrannical; and between himself and the page there goes on a strain of playfulness, in which his rollicking jokes appear to conceal an underlying vein of gentleness and tenderness. He is a big, fat, easy-going, easy-living man, who is not unkind, but *will* be indulged; who can bear much scolding, and yet is liked by those who scold him the loudest and with the most justice; a jovial, joyous, care-hating man, who will not beg pardon of the world for being in it; and who, moreover, thinks that the world ought to keep him well while it has him.

As it is, then, we take him for what he is, and accept the pleasure he affords. He does not arouse our antipathies, and he does not falsify our expectations. He is open and clear to our view, and we know him as he is; we do not look for moral greatness in him, as we do not require him to walk a thousand miles successively in a thousand hours. We should never mistake him for a peripatetic philosopher, and we feel no anger because he is not. As little should we mistake him for a patriot or a philanthropist. We should have had no hope, did he live in our age, to see him volunteer in the Greek war, or a missionary to the heathens of India. We should despair to move his heart to subscribe a cent to the Bible Society. Believing merely in this world, he would have no care beyond his own term of possession. With the Irishman in the house on fire, he would probably exclaim, What is it to me? I am but a tenant. Go to, go to, (he would say,) annoy me not with these vain disturbances; let your melancholy bipeds take such things in charge; let your lean folks see to them; let your restless, attenuated apologies for humanity, that have no appetite and no digestion, busy themselves with your spiritual irritations; but leave an honest man in peace, who understands what is good, and who knows how to use it.

To lay aside levity of expression, earnest purpose is foreign to characters of the Falstaff order. Seriousness, for good or evil, is no part of their nature; and if we laugh at their wit, it is with no approbation of their vices. We may relax with the indolent, and yet not depart from the worthy; we may contemplate a humorous phase of human nature, and though we do not resist the mirth which it excites, neither need we turn from it without some addition to our wisdom.

And this remark applies, I think, with very peculiar force to any intelligent reflection on the character of Falstaff. What a mournful condition of humanity is presented to us in the debasement of talent to the appetites! Behold it in the picture set before us in Falstaff! Look at that gray-headed, gray-bearded old man, lolling, bloated on the dregs of life; the desires insatiate as strength declines; the senses gross, while a brilliant imagination flows in radiance over them, as the sun upon a morass; abilities, which might have exalted empires, devoted to the cooking of a capon or the merits of a sack-posset; eloquence and wit lavished upon blackguards; law, honor, courage, chastity, made a jest. Laugh, it is true, you may; but, when you have laughed, turn back and think; and after thinking, you will admit that tragedy itself has not any thing more sad.

In the character of Falstaff there is a foregone conclusion, upon which every thoughtful mind will dwell. He is presented to us an old man, "written down old, with all the characters of age." We have, therefore, before us the last stage of a life, and we have its ultimate result. Were we to meet, in actual intercourse, a man with the genius and habits of Falstaff, we would know that a miserable experience lay behind it. The brilliant wit of the antiquated libertine might, for a moment, cause us to forget the purpose of existence, but soon, the bloated spectre would become to us its most solemn memento. Much, we would know, of excellent living material had been spoiled, ere the ruin which we gazed on could exist. There was a youth to this old age. We are sure that commanding abilities enriched it, for, even in their last abuse, these abilities are yet commanding; and truth, as it is now, could not always have been a jest. By what process, we would ask, has the noble been changed into the base? By a process, alas, too often repeated ever to be strange! There was fine judgment, but it was not under the guidance of rectitude. There was imagination, but it was not chastened by purity. There was sensibility, but it fell amidst grosser pleasures, and among them it was smothered. The merely intellectual faculties kept their supremacy, and the passions went from strength to strength. In the midst of boon companions, the royalty of sheer mind was acknowledged. The discourse of a strong reason compelled respect, even through the shoutings of revelry. The corruscations of a fire-lit fancy played among the broken clouds of nightly orgies, and tinted their ragged fringes with golden light. Days there were, which excitement shortened, and nights which gayety prolonged. While the senses had the illusion of an immortality in youth, pleasure appeared perennial; it seemed to have a fairness which could never wither, to flourish with a summer bloom which no frost could chill. Years wore on, the physical powers grew sluggish, and the mental powers selfish. At this stage of his course, let us suppose that we have such a person in the character of Falstaff. He has come to a dishonored and to a comfortless age. The world owes him no reverence. Mankind is indebted to such a man for nothing but his example; and for his example, only as a warning. He has been untrue to the affections, and now he has no affections true to him. Old, unwieldy, infirm, wifeless, childless, friendless, he is at last alone, among the dishonest, the degraded, and the false.

A sad life is that which is called a life of pleasure; and it is immeasurably sad when the sons of genius enslave themselves to it. How often must remorse appal them! What alternations to them of anguish and lassitude! What nights of madness, and what days of sorrow! Oh, how terrible to think of the past, when the past is an ocean overhung with darkness, and the shipwrecked faculties tossed in fragments upon its waves! Take into your mental view some voluptuary, who might have been an ornament to his species, but whom the infatuation of the senses has destroyed. Behold him in a moment of repentance and in solitude. Mark the wretchedness of his face and the convulsions of his breast. Look at him in his joyless home, where ruin is gathering to its last desolation, where hearts are throbbing which must soon be broken. For a little, the man, the generous, the loving man, seems to triumph in his nature; a new life seems to spring forth in his weeping, the return of an alienated heart to its allegiance, of a wandering soul to its peace, and a light of joy begins to overspread his dwelling. Watch him again encircled by his companions ; watch him, amused by the clashings of intoxicated eloquence ; whirled in the mazes of a delirious imagination ; the fatal spell comes over him again ; he gives himself to the trance with his eyes open, and the next time he awakes, he awakes to his perdition.

The law of compensation operates with certainty, and it operates impartially. To this solemn fact our great dramatist is ever faithful. This august poet of conscience and the heart, this wonderful revealer of the passions and their struggles, this moralist of insight, almost of inspiration, never forgets the eternal principles of right and wrong. In Falstaff, even as in Macbeth, Shakspeare vindicates these principles. Falstaff is loosely related to other men ; other men are, therefore, loosely related to him. He does not reap attachment where he has only sown indifference. His creed is turned on himself. He has no faith in excellence, and he gets no credit for possessing any. His practice is retorted as well as his creed. He uses his inferiors, and his superiors use *him*. They give him their presence when it is their desire to be amused, but they discard him as a worn rag when gayety is no longer seemly. Falstaff occasions mirth, but does not gain esteem. He adds to the brightness of the revel, but when the revel is over he is paid by no gratitude. For the vile there can be no esteem. Esteem cannot be where there is no confidence ; and there can be no confidence where there is no respect. The pure cannot have respect for the vicious ; and the vicious have no respect for each other. Their association precludes all reverence, for it is a cohesion in common infamy. They tolerate each other upon a mutual suppression of moral distinctions ; but there are times, when the bad appear to the bad more detestable than they possible can to the upright. The upright look not on the worst of their brethren without a touch of mercy ; but the bad, under the laceration of their crimes, glare upon their compeers with unmitigated horror. The bonds which keep them together are as fragile as they are corrupt, and when low interest or depraved gratification is exhausted, always easy to be severed. The vicissitude which breaks up the combination finds in every brother of it a traitor or an enemy. When once, therefore, a man plunges into a gross existence, he will, in time, discover that even the lowest will not do him reverence. He will be rejected by the persons who basked in the radiance of his fancy, and who were electrified by the flashes of his wit. Approbation is not for great talents, but for good works. Wages belong to the laborer, not to the idler, and much less to the spendthrift. It is no matter for praise that a man has a strong intellect, which is active only in debasement; that he has an affluence of imagination, which is squandered in corruption; that he has a rich faculty of eloquence, which is dumb on every generous theme and absent from all worthy places, which is only to be heard among inebriate debaters, and is only to be aroused by maudlin applause. No glory is for this man but shame, and shame the more burning for his genius.

The end of Falstaff may stand as a type for the close of every such life. It was without regret and without honor. There is no life so melancholy in its close, as that of a licentious wit. The companions with whom he jested abandon him; the hope of the visible world is gone, and in the spiritual he has no refuge. Utterly impoverished in all means of amusement and comfort, he is thrown entirely on himself; and, when he can least bear to be alone, he is delivered over to unmitigated solitude. Pleasure was the bond by which he held his former associates, and by affliction that bond is broken. The gay assembly takes no thought of him, and the place therein shall know him no more. Instead of the hilarious looks which were wont to beam around him, a crowd of ghastly images are flitting in his solitary room; instead of a board groaning under the weight of the feast, a couch is made hard with the pressure of disease; instead of the blaze of many lights, there is the dimness of a single taper; and for the song and the viol, there are the moanings of death.

Laurence Sterne had sentiment, which was often expressed with the most delicate tenderness, but he debased the finest of humor by the grossest of ribaldry. He scattered about him the wit of Rabelais, and his filth also; but when his brilliant career was run, there were none to cheer him at the end. "The last offices," Sir Walter Scott tells us, "were rendered him, not in his own house, or by kindred affection, but in an inn, and by strangers." Sir Walter also remarks, that Sterne's death strikingly resembled Falstaff's. Brinsley Sheridan was, like Falstaff, companion to a Prince of Wales. He was, also, like Falstaff, "a fellow of infinite jest, of most excellent fancy." He lavished upon this heir of kings the bounties of his humor and his eloquence, and in return for such wealth, the heir of kings abandoned the donor. When the lights went out upon the banquet, the man who threw the glory over it was no more remembered. But, when the frame sickened and the soul drooped, no royalty was at hand; when the eye had no more the lustre of wit, it looked in vain for brothers of the feast; when lips, from which there once flew winged words, feebly stammered titled names, none who bore those names were present to hear. The spendthrift, both in property and talents, was left alone with fate; and while eternity was opening for his spirit, the bailiffs were watching for his corpse.

The late Theodore Hook had vast capacities for amusing, and he, too, was a favorite with nobles and with princes. His repartees banished dulness from their parties, and his pen was the slave of their order. He was equally the champion of their politics, and the glory of their dinner tables. He was, in fact, a wit of all-work in aristocratic houses. He played, jested, conversed; tried, by every device, to make himself generally useful to his entertainers, and he was not unsuccessful. His brain was a storehouse of combustibles, out of which he played off intellectual fire-works in every caprice of oddity; his listless spectators gazed and admired, retired when the exhibition was over, and forgot the show. Meanwhile, secret wretchedness was devouring this man's life, and outward ruin was collecting on his head. He had gone through the experience of his class; he outran his means, depended on those whom he had amused, and found it was reliance upon a vapor. His comicry was all they wanted; they could afford him laughter, but not sympathy; they could join in his merriment, but they had no concern in his distress. His death was sudden, it was silent, and it was in poverty; "*He died, and made no sign!*"

This class is well embodied in Falstaff, in his life, also in his death. No death in Shakspeare is more sadly impressive to me than that of Falstaff. In the other deaths there is the sweetness of innocence, or the force of passion. Desdemona expires in her gentleness; Hamlet, with all his solemn majesty about him; Macbeth reels beneath the blow of destiny; Richard, in the tempest of his courage and his wickedness, finds a last hour conformable to his cruel soul; Lear has at once exhausted life and misery; Othello has no more for which he can exist; but the closing moments of Falstaff are gloomy without being tragic; they are dreary and oppressive, with little to relieve the sinking of our thoughts, except it be the presence of humanity in the person of Mrs. Quickly. When prince and courtier had forsaken their associate, this humble woman remained near him. The woman, whose property he squandered, and whose good name he did not spare; this woman, easily persuaded and easily deceived, would not quit even a worthless man in his helpless hour, nor speak severely of him when that hour was ended. Here is the greatness of Shakspeare: he never forgets our nature, and in the most unpromising circumstances he compels us to feel its sacredness. The last hours even of Falstaff he enshrouds in the dignity of death; and, by a few simple and pathetic words in the mouth of his ignorant but charitable hostess, he lays bare the mysterious struggles of an expiring soul. "'A parted," she says, "even just between twelve and one, e'en at turning o' the tide; for after I saw him fumble with the sheets, and play with flowers, and smile upon his fingers' ends, I knew there was but one way; for his nose was as sharp as a pen, and 'a babbled of green fields. How now, Sir John? quoth I: What, man! be of good cheer. So 'a cried out, God, God, God! three or four times; . . . then all was cold."

Thus, as Shakspeare pictures, a man of pleasure died. Even upon him nature again exerts her sway; the primitive delights of childhood revisit his final dreaming; and he plays with flowers, and he babbles of green fields. And that voice of eternal Power, which was lost in the din of the festival, must have utterance in the travail of mortality; and exclamations, which falter to the silence of the tomb, make confession of a faith which all the practice had denied.

CRABBE.

BEFORE proceeding to speak on the poetry of Crabbe, which forms the subject of the present Lecture, allow me to make some brief allusion to his life.

The Rev. GEORGE CRABBE was born in Aldborough, in 1754. Aldborough is a seacoast village of Suffolk, on the border of the German Ocean. His parents were in straitened circumstances, and he soon entered on a youth of hard condition and severe distress. His father, a man of strong intellect, had the sagacity to perceive the son's abilities, and, what little his narrow means afforded, he gave to aid their cultivation. Partly by intervals of schooling, but mainly by his own exertions, George acquired the rudiments of English and the classics. With this imperfect instruction, he was bound apprentice to a surgeon. His first master was a tyrant and an ignoramus, and from him he endured all sorts of injury, oppression, and insult. He finished his course with another, and he was more of a Christian and a gentleman.

In the mean time, he wrote verses in magazines, and, like all bards since the deluge, he fell in love. Surely this business of poor poets falling in love is a great folly under the sun. If they would be content to court the Muses with Platonic wooing, they might have our forbearance; these gentle creatures can eat ambrosia with the gods, and drink water from Helicon. But when the sons of Parnassus, who have only kingdoms in the stars and castles in the clouds, presume to damsels, who need more solid sustenance than moonshine, they are guilty of most heinous crime, and if common sense were judge, they should undergo their due desert without mitigation and without mercy. But as things are managed, the rogues escape; they tell women they are angels; these angels are women, and believe them. It is, however, but the common fashion of the world, and, whether in prose or rhyme, the history of men and maidens is the same to the end of the chapter. Crabbe rejoiced in his magazine and his mistress; they were no bad things to rejoice in, and they were all he had.

Thus he arrived at that point of manhood, when all who were not provided with hereditary fortune, must enter on some settled mode of labor. He returned to the house of his parents with at least the name of a profession. Either, however, from want of skill, or want of sphere, his profession served him to little purpose, and for a period he was not only a burden to his home, but a burden very unwillingly endured. The character of his father had undergone a melancholy change. His father had been always poor; his principal support was a humble government situation, connected with a tax at that time on salt; his income was scanty, and his temper had become unamiable; to poverty and bad temper, he added the habits of a tippler, and any leisure that his employment allowed, he spent in surly indolence in his house, or in boisterous carousals in the tavern.

Of sensitive spirit and independent character, George felt his situation a bitter bondage; and, sooner than eat the bread of idleness, he often became his father's porter, and carried sacks from the vessels to the warehouse. In the intervals of chagrin and labor, he was not unmindful of his darling pursuits; and of these intervals two complete poems were the result—"The Village," and "The Library." With these he determined to go to London, and to London he went. Once there, his whole stock consisted of a very scanty wardrobe and three pounds in money. Simple as Fielding's Parson Adams, his manuscripts seemed to him a mine of wealth, but booksellers returned them to him unread: and when, with better hopes, he presented them to the wealthy, liveried lackeys, after a few days, handed them back with an insolent version of their masters' cold refusal.

In the mean time, he was reduced to forlorn indigence. Credit with his landlady was all but exhausted, his wardrobe was in pawn, a meal had become rare, and a roof uncertain. In the extremity of wretchedness, by a happy inspiration, he wrote to the celebrated orator, Edmund Burke. The letter was eloquent — worthy of a man, and a man of genius. The poet called; the orator received him with courteous generosity. The interview, as described by Mr. Crabbe's filial biographer, is an honor to the poet and the politician. As alike creditable to literature and human nature, I extract it:

"Mr. Burke was at this period (1781) engaged in the hottest turmoils of parliamentary opposition, and his own pecuniary circumstances were by no means very affluent; yet he gave instant attention to this letter, and the verses which it inclosed. He immediately appointed an hour for my father to call upon him at his house in London; and the short interview which ensued, entirely and forever changed the nature of his fortunes. He was, in the common phrase, 'a made man' from that hour. He went into Mr. Burke's room a poor, young adventurer, spurned by the opulent and rejected by the publishers, his last shilling gone, and all but his last hope with it; he came out virtually secure of almost all the good fortune, that by successive steps afterwards fell to his lot; his genius acknowledged by one whose verdict could not be questioned; his character and manners appreciated and approved by a noble and capacious heart, whose benevolence knew no limits but its power—that of a giant intellect, who was in feeling an unsophisticated child — a bright example of the close affinity between superlative talents and the warmth of generous affections."

Burke took the poet, pale and shabby as he was, to his country seat, at Beaconsfield, and there he gave him a sanctuary for his studies and a refuge from his wants. He gained him friends, procured him ordination in the Church of England, obtained for him a chaplaincy with the Duke of Rutland, and lost no sight of him until the grave drew the curtain which shuts out earth with all its wisdom as well as all its vanities. Thenceforth success waited on his poetry, and promotion on his priesthood; fortune smiled upon them both. The remainder of a long life was all that a wise man could desire. Through a great portion of it he had for his companion the woman of his youthful choice; his children were what his piety and love could wish; plenty abounded within his gates, and peace governed his household. Of pitiful and kindly heart, of simple, unsophisticated manners, he had the affection of the poor and the esteem of the noble. He went down to a good old age with a poet's fame, and he lay upon a death-bed with a Christian's hope. His life, admirably and modestly written by his son, I would recommend to my youthful hearers as a fine lesson of patience, piety, and wisdom.

In reading such stories as Crabbe's, we cannot think of his trials in London, without recalling some of his literary predecessors: we recall Samuel Johnson and David Garrick tramping thither on foot, having on their arrival three pence halfpenny between them; we recall that same Johnson, — that unwieldy mass of spleen and benevolence, of eloquent thought and childish superstition, toiling through heroic years, constant to his noble task, in long, unnoticed, and unrewarded labor. Yet there was that in those meditations of destitute genius which shortened the hours of poverty; a glory and a joy which brightened the unpictured walls of the garret; a sweetness of virtue on the hard, rough bed, which forsakes the couches of the proud. We recall also the hapless Richard Savage, strolling after midnight to the refuge of some familiar shed;

poor Boyce stiffened in his blanket; unhappy Otway choked with his penny loaf; and youthful Chatterton, by his own dismissal, sent to his last and dread account. These are but a few noted victims who have left names, from the thousands who never had any.

How many cast themselves on the terrible experiment of a literary life in London, who are never more to be heard of! How many starve where they expected fortune, and find obscurity where they hoped for fame! How many wear out existence in abortive efforts, exhaust their enthusiasm in alternations of expectance and despondency; behold the beams which lingered longest vanish from the most distant verge of the horizon; then, close their career in madness, or drop their unknown being into the gulf of everlasting oblivion! Where are the throngs of ardent and exultant men, who yearly point their tracks towards the living wilderness, but show no traces of return? Perhaps a sister, in a distant province, weeps upon her nightly pillow for an absent brother; perhaps a mother holds her son in holy thoughts, and recalls him in her speechless prayer; but haply, in some sunless den of literary poverty, he has departed in silence to his eternal home!

The literary life, like the military, holds a thousand promises to the ear, which must be broken to the hope; like the military, it is in fancy all bright and joyous, with no gleam in the future but the blaze of glory, and no cloud upon its light, but the flag of victory ; like the military too, on the other side, it is in the reality to the multitude of aspirants an experience of toil, danger, an anxious life, an obscure death; and instead of a sun rising high upon their path, opening to them a wide horizon, and filling it with the gladness of their fame, they have the scorching heat of a weary day ; and the shadow, which at a distance, they pictured as the banner of their triumph, they find upon advancing, often to be only the dimness of a garret or the blackness of their grave. The scholar, like the soldier, pants for distinction, and in the scholar it is a desire as humane as it is profound; it is a generous desire, and yet it can be but rarely gratified.

Men must content themselves to work and be forgotten. They must work on, work well, work faithfully ; and then, when their labor is finished, be satisfied to go into the fathomless and the everlasting silence. The past as it recedes sinks into benevolent oblivion ; and nature mercifully prepares a new world for others as they come. The grass has been scarcely ten times renewed upon our graves, when neighbors forget who sleep beneath them ; and the fate of men is that of writings. Every large library we enter, and every olden folio we open, reminds us of the facility with which the world forgets; it is, in fact, the great winnowing process, whereby the true seed of thought is preserved, that would otherwise rot in accumulating rubbish.

The diffusion of knowledge, also, which characterizes our age, whilst it has increased the demand for literature, has also, in a much larger degree, multiplied the candidates for its distinctions. Reputation becomes more and more difficult of attainment, and if attained, more and more transient and uncertain of possession. Literature, therefore, as a field for glory, is an arena where a tomb may be more easily found than laurels; as a means of support, it is the very chance of chances.

These remarks have peculiar force in reference to poetry. Mediocrity of bardship is held fatal; it is doubly cursed; it can procure neither fame nor food; if sing it must, the crowd will not stop to listen, and while it sings it starves. In other days, poetic mediocrity was not utterly hopeless; a lord who longed for praise, found a minstrel who wanted bread; the peer swallowed the yearly ode, and the poet devoured his daily loaf. Mediocrity ate its venal portion in content, but genius took it with bitterness; the one warbled away comfortably in the cage of patronage, the other drooped its pinions, or smashed them against the bars; the one is now broken on the blast of an open public opinion, the other mounts proudly upon the tempest and rises to the sun.

In criticism which is not merely literary, but moral also, it will not seem inappropriate to refer to influences which create poetry such as Crabbe's, and to tendencies which it indicates.

The concerns of humble life are the principal topics on which our poet dwells; but, though in Crabbe they are distinctive, they have a prominent position in all the modern literature of English life. Sympathy is in others; reality in Crabbe. Goldsmith has idealized the rural village in his lambent fancy and his melodious verse; he deceives us into delight; and from childhood to old age, as Sir Walter Scott has said, we return to him with a new desire, to his gentle pathos, that moves the heart without storming the passions; to his happy style, that wins attention without solicitation, that never taxes, and that never tires. The description of a poor country girl in the metropolis, towards the close of "The Deserted Village," is a picture of lowly tragedy, which Crabbe might have conceived and painted.

Many others I might name, but I pass on to Cowper. Cowper, yet more than Goldsmith, had strong sympathies with the trials of the English poor. He was peculiarly fitted, by his simple habits and benignant genius, to take a strong interest in the concerns of lowly life. The objects amidst which he lived, and of which he loved to write, were, for the most part, unpretending and retired; the shaded walk, the neat-trimmed garden, the sunny corner, the nest of flowers, the grassy valley and the woodland hill, the social parlor, the cheerful winter fire. From these, and such things as these, the loving heart extracted a poetry which cannot fail of readers, while goodness has any place in letters, while the grace of purity can give comeliness to human speech. The poor man's labors and the poor man's cares, were with him in his familiar thoughts; he paints, with true hand and inspired eye, the poor man's home, the virtues and the pleasures of his fireside, the sanctity of his domestic altar, the beauty of humble holiness, the griefs and the joys that lie along the path of laborious life. Of all writers, he is the most sinless in wit and humor. What others turn to ribaldry or gall, he "turns to prettiness;" in expression, polished and effective; in fancy, playful, chaste, rich; he stirs up mirth from the very bottom of the heart, until the shaking sides are tired and the laughing eyes are dim, yet in no word or hint does he leave a trace upon the soul which could shame the holiest memory in its holiest hour. Pungent but not envenomed, uncompromising but not uncharitable, grave in truth, gentle in ridicule, he makes nothing odious but sin, and nothing laughable but folly.

Poetry such as this, and such as Crabbe's, is the creation of Christianity. It is the result of interests which Christianity has developed, and of sympathies which it has inspired. Christianity has opened springs of joy and sorrow before untouched ; it has called new and unimagined agencies into being. Man has received a redemption from contempt. It may not always save man from wrong, but it guards him from scorn ; much he may be made even now to suffer, but he can never be as he was, despised. By the glory it gives the soul, the lowly and the poor have gained importance, and with importance they have risen to a history and a literature.

The laboring classes of ancient nations afforded no scope for poetry, no materials for story. In the universal vassalage which brooded over Pagan States, no ideal interest could pertain to the unprivileged masses. There was nothing in the laughter or the tears of the multitude, to command attention or dignify description ; nothing to give embellishment to the feast, or gain an audience at the games. What was it to the proud and mighty, what was it to the learned and the brave, what was it to the philosophers of academy or the philosophers of porch, where helots lived or how helots died ? But Christianity, in its revelation of a spiritual and immortal being, has given man an infinite worth ; it has enriched him with an endowment independent of social distinctions, and transcendently superior to them. In restraining the passions, it has diversified and raised them; in exalting woman, it has created the poetry of domestic life; in ennobling every destiny, it has deepened and complicated all the tragic elements of our nature; it has sublimed the catastrophe, both of good and evil; the good with a holier joy, and the evil with a gloomier sadness.

In beauty of forms, in harmonies of language, in incidents of romance, our times certainly cannot compete with ages that are gone; but, assuredly, the poetry of those departed ages, is more desirable than their practice. Greece and Rome, in their classical period, present, to our retrospective imaginations, a vista of most wondrous glory. We behold them in remote and majestic serenity, with the sun of an enchanting loveliness lingering over them; we behold them in fragments of art, unapproachable and unrivalled; we behold them in a long array of statues, temples, columns, but, while we muse delighted, we recall not the butcheries of the circus; we are charmed with the music of noblest eloquence and divinest poetry, but while we are raptured with such harmonies, we hear not the groans of dying gladiators, we hear not the rabble-yells which drowned them, we come not in contact with slaveries wide almost as the world, that called forth no pity, and knew no hope ; we comprehend with no adequate conception, the wilderness of evil which the gloom of heathenism covered ; the dark destinies which a ray from heaven scarcely pierced ; the wretchedness unsolaced, and the sin unrebuked ; which fancy shudders to paint, and faith is unwilling to believe.

Europe, in the middle ages, has its glory too ; a glory that deludes us with many fascinations. A picturesque and romantic splendor overspreads these ages, but the obscurity which gives them mystic grandeur to our fancies, hides their evils from our disgust. Belted knight and baron bold, will be ever fine in story ; we call them up in their strength and bravery ; we not only reanimate them with a new life of resurrection, but we clothe them with a new light of transfiguration. In this, as in all things, the beautiful is immortal, the bad has perished. These men rise up before us in their chivalric and heroic deeds, but the witnesses of their crimes do not come so quickly ; the serfs whom they trampled, are nameless and numberless in the dust of centuries ; the cries of their midnight murders have passed to as deep a silence as the laughter of their midnight revels ; the eyes which they caused to weep, have long closed in final slumber, and the hearts which they crushed, are quiet in eternal rest. A poetry of the poor, which must necessarily be a moral poetry, a poetry of sentiment and sympathy, has no alliance with the gorgeousness of chivalric times ; and the physical luxuriance and voluptuous personification, which belonged to Pagan mythology, have no congruity with modern poetry.

Poetry must embody faith, or it is an empty sound. Our faith has not taken the material universe from poetry, but it has changed their relations. We have not a distinct deity for every region of nature ; every object to us does not present an embodied god ; we see no goddess blush in the morning's dawn ; we behold no divinity clothing himself with light in the rising sun ; we hear no celestial anger in the tempest of the winds and the roaring of the seas ; we see no gods at peace in the serene calm of the blue sky, and the gladsome quiet of the verdant earth ; we have no vision of naïad or nymph, by stream or fountain, in glen or cavern.

And, it is not, as I have said, that creation is empty, or that poetry has deserted nature. The same beautiful nature is with us, as with the ancients ; around us, as around the men of other days, around Wordsworth as around Homer, around Bryant as around Hesiod. Ages have not dimmed the sun, nor dried up from the stars their rivers of light. The same glorious temple is above us, and the same gorgeous floor beneath us; the desert has still its spots of Eden, the sky has still its palaces of cloud, the universe is still the same, but the "gods many and the lords many," which bewildered fancy fashioned, have dissolved before enlightened reason. One God and one Lord reigns upon the throne; the King eternal and immortal, sways the sceptre of the worlds, and commands the homage of their worship; one spirit moves and lives in all; one spirit guides and governs all. The ocean mirrors his immensity, the thunder shouts his praise; cataracts, in the mighty wilderness, foam perennial incense; the hills are his everlasting altars, and all the elements are his ministers. Hence our literature — above all, our poetry — has not only a more exalted inspiration, but a more expansive interest; the poor have their importance as the rich, for Jehovah has made them both, and before Jehovah both are equal.

Crabbe is the *poet* of poverty; but perhaps that may be too fine a name; let us then call him the *metrical historian* of the poor. Among our moral poets, Crabbe, as the critics admit, is the most original, — the most original in topics, thoughts, and style. His works stand alone in English literature; and yet their peculiarity is their truth, and not their invention; the rigor of reality, and not the witcheries of fancy. The objects of humble life are not with Crabbe, as they are with Wordsworth, mere occasions of philosophic musings; not forms that glide dimly in the world of dreams, but creations of flesh and blood, that dwell amidst the wants and cares of earth.

Crabbe, in his sphere, is independent and unaided. A Columbus in descriptive and didactic poetry, he discovered a wild and wide region; he traversed it to its utmost limits, and made it his own, irrevocably and forever. Hardy and alone in his explorings, he has no traditional guidance, and he seeks no sympathy from romantic imagination. In the unbeaten wilderness to which he pierced, he found no inherited domains, venerable with centuries of ancestral woods; no gray abbeys, whose bells had tolled before the curfew; no dark-walled castles, whose courts, in olden times, had rung with the tramp of warriors; no heroines or heroes, no fair ladies or brave knights, no chivalry or crusading, no giants or wizards, no pilgrims or saints; none of these were of the world which he chronicled; but a population unknown in story, a population of hard labor and hard life, of lowly dwellings and of nameless graves. He revealed, with austere minuteness, the secrets that he found; he opened the concealments of poverty and crime; he entered the alms-house, the prison, the dwellings of the over-taxed and over-toiling poor, and he detailed, with pertinacious veracity, the history of their inmates. Like the "Ancient Mariner" of Coleridge, he stopped the guests on the threshold of their luxurious feast; by a ruthless magic he chained their attention to his terrible narrations; compelled them to hear his tale of "Life in Death;" that life pining away in death, in the midst of a dreary sea to which his listeners had never pierced.

The poems of Crabbe may be classed under three distinct designations, as tragic, moral, and satirical; and, by the laws that respectively govern these, we must regulate our criticism and form our decision. If we regard Crabbe as a tragic writer, we must not complain that he is gloomy; if we take him as a moralist, we must not wonder at his severity; if we turn to him as a satirist, we must expect often to find him bitter or sarcastic.

Crabbe is a writer of harrowing, tragic power; his narratives are so vivid, as almost to be dramatic; you not only follow the incidents of a story, but you conceive the presence of an action. He lays bare the human heart, and shows the loves and hatreds, the vices and the virtues, that work within it, the agonies and fears that wreck and break it. He observes the passions in their modifications, he traces them in all their stages, he portrays them in all their consequences;

the love that lingers guileless to the grave, or shivers the brain in madness; the revenge that never quits its deadly thought, until it is perfected in the horrid deed; the remorse that follows sin, that haunts the affrighted conscience through existence.

Never has didactic poet more effectively than Crabbe, exhibited his teachings in dramatic example. His characters are drawn with such fidelity, that you behold them with all their living peculiarities. In both the description of scenes and the portraiture of characters, we observe evidence of mournful thoughtfulness, of accurate inspection; of scrupulous reality, of careful coloring.

Fishermen and smugglers are frequently his personages, and with these, and their fortunes, he constantly links descriptions of the ocean which are fearful and sublime. With ruthless fidelity, he paints dreary portions of the shore with most mournful accessories; the desert beach; the chilly and the slimy strand; muscle-gatherers prowling through the mud; smugglers preparing to brave the tempest and the deep; wreckers watching for their prey. Taking a barren field adjacent to the sea, by a few salient touches,—such as a ragged child torn by brambles, a group of scattered hats, a company of gypsies, a straggling poacher, a gaudy weed, a neglected garden,—he will make a picture of sadness, that shall oppress you as a thing of sense.

His style corresponds to his thoughts; austere and simple, he entrusts entirely to the naked force of meaning, and that meaning it is impossible to mistake. The wickedness of sin, the wreck of passion, appear more fearful when they are not so much described as displayed by this colorless language, which, like the cloudless atmosphere, exhibits objects, without exhibiting itself. Minuteness of touch is the characteristic which critics commonly attribute to the moral pictures of Crabbe. Generally, this may be correct, yet no writer can suggest more than Crabbe does, at times, in few words, as where he describes the lady,

> "wise, austere, and nice,
> Who showed her virtue, by her scorn of vice;"

Or, when he sets before us the pliant parson, who pleased his parishioners by never offending them; one of those good easy souls, who never know the loss of appetite by the toils of thought; who bow and smile, and always say "yes;" whom an independent opinion would frighten, as a ghost from the dead; and who would as soon mount a forlorn hope, as venture on a sturdy contradiction.

> "Fiddling and fishing were his arts; at times
> He altered sermons, and he aimed at rhymes."

Crabbe's poetry is the tragedy of common life, and as tragedy we must judge it. The tragic elements are in rude forms as well as ideal ones; they are in humble conditions as well as in heroic situations. They belong to human nature in its essence, and the modes in which they show themselves are but the accidents of art or circumstances. The tragic genius naturally selects the sad and the terrible in our nature; most poets have associated these elements with exalted condition or extraordinary events. Crabbe has connected them with lowly individuals and unromantic incidents. If we, therefore, call Crabbe gloomy, why should we not so designate every writer who is purely tragic? Does Crabbe, in his terrible scenes, intend to give a general picture of common life? No, assuredly. He no more intends this, than the writer of romantic tragedy intends to represent his impersonations as the veracity of history, or as the counterparts of elevated rank. Crabbe, most certainly would no more imply that Peter Grimes, a vulgar, but gloomy and atrocious man was common among fishermen, than Massinger would have it understood that Sir Giles Overreach was a frequent character among private gentlemen. Peter Grimes is in essence a tragic character, as well as Sir Giles Overreach. In what sense, then, is Crabbe a gloomy writer in which Massinger is not also? Is it that the personages of Crabbe are of low or every-day existence?

Whether these are proper subjects for tragic story is a question of criticism, that I cannot here discuss, and the discussion of it is not necessary to my subject. The *condition* of the characteristics does not in any way affect the spirit which they embody. Admitting much of nature in that sympathy with the sorrows of those raised above us, which we so strongly feel, I think there is also in it somewhat of prejudice. Feelings more genuine and more true, would teach us not to destroy the difference but to lessen it. Some persons can feel for woe that weeps amidst gauze and gas light, and faints most gracefully in a spangled robe, while they will turn away in disgusted selfishness from vulgar want. Yet the record of such want, the knowledge that such want has being, ought more to touch our hearts than the genteelest agony that was ever printed upon vellum. Sensibility, which is moral rather than imaginative, which has its glow in the affections, rather than in the fancy, can approach rude suffering in its coarseness, and it can bear it in description.

Crabbe dispelled many illusions which the fiction and falsehood of our literature had maintained in reference to humble life. Nor was it unkindness to the poor, but rather benevolence, to dispel such deceptions. The region of laborious life was, to poets and their patrons, an enchanted Eden; a fairy land, where some light from the golden age continued yet to linger; where passions were asleep, where tastes were simple, and where wants were few. The bards sang sweetly of poverty with blessed content; of innocence in rural vales, of shepherds that only dreamed of love, and hinds that whistled as they went for want of thought; of swains that tuned their oaten pipes, and maidens that listened in rapture to the sound; well pleased, the wealthy heard; sure never was lot so happy as the poor enjoyed; and while crime and misery were at their doors, they read only of contented Louisas and gentle Damons; then rushed to ball and banquet in the bliss of ignorance, and without one pang of charity.

Crabbe revealed other matters. He showed that sin and sorrow, guilt and passion, are doing their work at the base of society, as well as on its summit; he showed that the heart was much the same history in all conditions. This, so far, was novelty; and surely the novelty of truth is worth something, even when it is not so pleasant as we might desire; nor is that power manifested in vain, which shows us that the fearful strength of human nature which wrecks a throne, may spend as terrible a fury on a cottage hearth.

As a matter of taste, we may object to the social grade of Crabbe's personages: as matter of principle, I see not that we can. Neither can we object to him that he connects them with dark and destructive passions. The passions are essentially the same, whether in high life or low; and with those which are dark and destructive the tragic writer deals, whether he places the catastrophe in palace or in tent. The envy of Iago, the jealousy of Othello, the ambition of Macbeth, and the cruelty of Richard, are all the same envy, jealousy, ambition, and cruelty in so many peasants; and in peculiarity of circumstances they might be equally as tragic. Will it be said, that Crabbe deals with such passions exclusively? It is not so; passages of greater sweetness, passages more loving, gentle, tender, beautiful, than numbers to be found in Crabbe, poet has seldom written. Take, for instance, the story of Phœbe Dawson; the sketch of the young girl towards the close of the "Parish Register," and her consumptive sailor lover; "The Parting Hour," and "Farmer Ellis;" and if they have not moral truth and beauty, strong and devoted affections, I do not know what can be considered truth, beauty, or affection.

Crabbe is not ungentle, but he is sad. He has not the genial amplitude of Burns, and neither his constitution nor his circumstances tended to produce it. Burns, with a rare affluence of soul, was trained among an intelligent, and, on the whole, independent population; with trials, to be sure, around them, that would often make them sad, but seldom the sordid wretchedness that could see no hope. Daily there was labor in the field, and sometimes there was sorrow on the hearth, but the cloud was not enduring; fun soon laughed at care again, and frolic danced as merrily as ever.

Crabbe in youth had but little pleasure; in London he was steeped in poverty to the very lips; in mature life his professional position, in neighborhoods abounding with destitution, brought him continually into contact with the most forlorn ignorance, and the most hapless vice. He does not often rise to the raptures of enjoyment, but he has constantly gleams of the beautiful in human life; the fidelities of lowly attachment; the sensibilities and the grace, that nature gives to an unperverted woman; the glory that, in the hardest fortune, crowns the brave and honest man.

I would not say, however, that Crabbe never presents too gloomy an aspect of existence. His pictures of poverty, with its attendant evils, are often certainly too harsh; often as partial as they are discolored; pictures which evince a fearful power of causing pain, but which afford no moral compensation for the agony they excite. This remark applies very extensively to most of our poet's views of external nature. His eye is sicklied with hues of sorrow, and his ear is disordered with its sounds. The burden of lamentation intercepts from his hearing the music of paradise; the sun sets with glory in the heavens, but while he gazes, a mist of tears ascends from earth to dim it; the flower rejoices in the desert, but man is trodden in the crowd; the stream is clear in the solitude, but in habitable places it is the mirror of worn faces and blasted forms. Our poet wanders too much like a haunted man, meeting at too many turns a gaunt and remorseless spectre of crime and suffering. Intervals of release he has; intervals of many genial thoughts, when the sounds of the living world, if melancholy, are at least musical; when human goodness and human affections throw their beauty on his dream, and when the sympathies of love, undimmed by selfishness, come pictured from his fancy in pencillings of light.

As a moralist, Crabbe is most solemn and most impressive. The power of his description is equalled only by his truth of principle and his moveless integrity of purpose. Never has moralist exhibited more terribly than Crabbe the maledictions that fall upon the guilty. Never has moralist exhibited the awful law of right and wrong, in so many and impressive forms. Wherever he places sin, there is the reign of misery — in the rural cottage, in the city garret, on the midnight ocean, on the barren moor. Wherever he gives us the crime, he gives us the retributive calamity, that dogs it with certain step, and strikes when the clock of fate has tolled the hour of execution. He makes no compromise ; he flatters no sin; he softens no sentence that it merits ; he conceals no consequence of ruin that follows it ; he confounds no distinctions of obligation ; he sophisticates no principles of action ; he loosens no bonds of duty ; he shakes no trust in virtue ; he wrings our hearts, but he warns them ; and while he moves us to sadness, he moves us to wisdom.

As a satirist, I do not remember much that I can commend in Crabbe. This aspect of his poetry is to me one of complete repulsion ; one of harshness, that inflicts pain, and does not minister to correction. Crabbe wanted the gayety of heart, which enables the satirist to please as well as to chastise ; he wanted that easy and sportive fancy, which adds grace even to censure ; he wanted that exhilarating humor, which can prevent anger from deepening to malice or contempt, by a joyous and a humanizing laugh. Our author's son commends his satire ; but satire does not, as I can perceive, suit either his temper or his subjects. His temper inclined him to the melancholy in our life and nature ; his manner is therefore so uniformly serious, that satire, in its levity, would sound from him like laughter in a church. The gravity of satire is still more inconsistent with his subjects.

The follies or the vices of the poor call for our pity or our grief, but not for our scorn or our smiles. In his poem of "The Borough," Crabbe is tremendously severe on players, and in his lacerating description of the poor strollers whom he satires, there is unquestionable power; but when power is turned against the weak and the helpless, every generous and pitying nature rebels against tyrannic genius. The most prosperous in the theatrical profession illustrate so strikingly the vicissitude and transiency of our human state, that I can connect them with only sober associations; the unsuccessful, whose work is hard, and whose pay is as uncertain as it is scanty, I can regard only with sadness and compassion. There is so much of the glare and grief of life connected with the stage, that it fills me with most solemn thoughts. To-day the god and goddess of the scene, stifled with crowds, inflated with applause, tread with ecstasy a giddy and an airy height; that height has been attained, often, through years of labor, trials, fears, want, and suffering; now wealth flows in upon them with most ample measure; plaudits hail their triumphs, and intoxicated joy is theirs to suffocation. All these will soon be gone and silent; a brief enthusiasm will give them to oblivion, or give them to the tomb.

I heard the wonderful Malibran in her latest concert. I listened to her dying song. She poured forth her impassioned soul, "in linked sweetness long drawn out," through all the mazes of music. A glorious crowd was before her of jewelled and joyous beauty; light and gladness gave enchantment to the hour, and thousands of excited hearts were raised to the delirium of delight. At this moment, life in her who caused the pleasure was throbbing to its close. Encore upon encore echoed in shouts that seemed to rend the ceiling. The poor singer came on, elated by the cheers; sustained by wonted fervor, her sinking form arose living and elastic; her transcendent eye kindled even with unusual fire; her magical tones swelled and sank, and floated into wilder ecstasy; again the building rang with plaudits — they were her triumph and her knell. I might have gone from this place to the stage door of the next theatre; and there I might have seen a weary creature, coming out from her night's unnoticed labor, and she was also going home to die. No praise cheered her spirit; no echoes, growing fainter, lingered on her ear; no soul the next evening would remark her absence, would care for her return. I might have seen a trembling girl, such as Crabbe, in the section I have mentioned, describes with a pathos that compensates for his severity towards the other members of her company. I might have seen this trembling girl, who, a moment before, was blazing in tinsel, amidst gas and gilding, stealing to her cold and shabby lodging; the paint washed from her cheek, and leaving the pallor of consumption in its stead; the mimic smile of gladness passed away, to be succeeded by real tears of nature; tears that now may flow in freedom, and flow in silence. Shame upon the soul, that could give her afflicted lot only a hard thought and a hard word; shame upon the pharisaism, that could discern no motive in her career but vanity, when charity, that "thinketh no evil," might suggest impulses more worthy, the necessities, perhaps, of a widowed mother, or a sickly father, or of helpless and orphaned brothers and sisters. Shame upon the unmanly insolence that impedes her way; shame upon the unmanly insult that crimsons her cheek; shame upon the dastardly sus picion, native to the meanness of a small soul, and to the filth of a corrupted heart, that supposes the unprotected always to be vicious, the poor to be without honor, and the weak to be proper objects of foul intentions.

I have given the character of Crabbe's poetry with all the fidelity of one who has read it with interest, and therefore read it with attention. Its special divisions I will now indicate, but cannot analyze. His two earliest poems were, " The Village," and " The Library." " The Village " has not the sweetness of Goldsmith, and " The Library " has not the learning of Parr ; but the one gained him the patronage of Burke ; the other was written under his roof, and obtained his approbation. " The Village " has power and pathos, but it is in stoic opposition to the Arcadian poetry on villages. " The Library " contains some quaint and amusing ideas on the matter, the size, and the destiny of books. It would surely be a droll circumstance to the authors of many folios, to arise from the dead and behold the nonentities to which they have sunk. How indignant they must feel to know that their immense tomes had only made small talk for D'Israeli, and banter for George Crabbe.

" The Parish Register " and " The Borough," were intermediate publications. They contain, however, all the essentials of Crabbe's genius, although he modified them afterwards, by shaping them into other poems, In " The Tales," Crabbe's power is concentrated and intense ; in the " Tales of the Hall," diversified and softened ; but still we find the same stoic description, and the same literal and inflexible pathos. Crabbe's pathos has an inveterate accuracy throughout ; you can never call it moonshine, and, to escape its pain, you must refuse to read. The reality you cannot contest. "The Parish Register" is drawn from his experience as a clergyman. It contains a large amount of reflection on the most solemn eras of individual history, "birth," "marriage," and "death." Generally, these pictures are sad, but with their sadness they have many hues of beauty; the smile of infancy as well as its suffering; the devotedness of maternity as well as its anguish; the affection of humble marriage as well as its afflictions; the peace of death as well as its fears; its triumphs as well as its despair.

The episode of "Phœbe Dawson" in this poem, has won enthusiastic applause from the critics; as its beauty and its pathos must have done, except critics had not hearts. It was one of the last things which Fox, that orator of manly soul, perused on his dying bed. Crabbe has been singularly fortunate in securing the appreciation of great men. Burke ushered him to notice; Fox read him in his last sickness; Byron regarded him with admiration; Scott revered him as a poet and a friend; and in the disconsolate hours which closed his mighty life, while able to study, he perused our poet's writings and the Bible.

"The Borough" is a poem of greater extent and of wider scope. It consists of those topics which an

English town affords ; and of such materials as almost only an English town can furnish. Among the subjects in which he shows the greatest force and skill, I would instance, " The Alms House," " The Prisons," and " The Dwellings of the Poor." Two melancholy pictures he gives us in " The Alms House ; " the poor outworn spendthrift, strutting still in fragments of olden finery ; the antique beauty, unable, through all the discipline of sorrow, to forget her conquests ; these we cannot contemplate without emotion. Much as we may despise folly that is proof against all experience, we cannot but feel for a weight of affliction that is too heavy, to allow even folly, to be always absurd. " The Prison " and its inmates, are described with especial power. In the dream of the condemned felon we have a fine illustration of the godliness of our nature, even in its guilt ; the gleams of tenderness that shoot across the dreary wastes of sin ; the recollection that transports the heavy heart from the starless night of its despair, to the sunny morning of its hope.

Alluding to " The Dwellings of the Poor," I would say that this is the special sphere in which Crabbe rules our feelings with a wizard and vindictive spell. In moral pathos, sometimes fearful, sometimes tender, his genius here becomes terrible and august. He leads us to homes of indigence, where the senses are gross, the passions mad ; where the affections are base or broken ; where the intellect made for heaven, is buried in the grossness of the brute ; where appetite holds undivided despotism ; where fancy sheds no light, and faith no purity, and hope no consolation ; where holiness has no sanctuary, and prayer no altar, and the Sabbath no sacrifice ; where the morning sun gilds no grateful offering, and the evening hears no vesper praise ; where intemperance makes a fiend of man, and cruelty a wreck of woman ; where an old age of wretchedness closes a life of vice ; where the weary spirit seeks a place to gasp its latest breath ; or where the forlorn skeleton sits sullen or stupefied on the unwilling hearth ; where beauty is turned to ashes ; the gladness and the glory of life departed ; the spirit broken and the soul forsaken. But it is not all thus in Crabbe's writings ; thank God, it is not all thus, in the poorest homes ; poverty has its limits of suffering, and sin its boundary of dominion ; even in the view of our unromantic poet, humble homes have light from heaven, that also guides to heaven ; sweetness of temper that no anguish can destroy ; a reverence and love of goodness that no temptation can corrupt ; charities undimned through years of struggle ; piety that no woe can shake ; patience, that, with a blessed alchemy, distils a balm from the most bitter wormwood of tribulation; piety that willingly, and with graceful word, bestows its mite, and sighs when it has no more to give.

I would, with very strong desire, illustrate, by quotations, all I have said of the poet whose genius I have undertaken to discuss; but time will not allow it.

That Crabbe, when he pleased, could rise far above the level of his usual plain and tranquil couplet, into the boldest diction and the most daring eloquence of the imagination, is evidenced in his tales of "Sir Eustace Grey" and "The Hall of Justice." In the one he treads through the darkest mazes of insanity; in the other he fathoms the utmost depths of misery and passion. In "Sir Eustace Grey," after the poet rings upon our ears all the wildering changes of a despairing insanity, how finely does he soften down those terrible ravings, and close in the sweet song of religious confidence and returning peace. Thus the patient sings:

"Pilgrim, burden'd with thy sin,
Come the way to Zion's gate,
There, till mercy let thee in,
Knock and weep, and watch and wait.
Knock! He knows the sinner's cry;
Weep! He loves the mourner's tears;
Watch! for saving grace is nigh;
Wait! till heavenly light appears.

"Hark! it is the Bridegroom's voice;
Welcome Pilgrim to thy rest;
Now within the gate rejoice,
Safe and seal'd, and bought and bless'd!
Safe — from all the lures of vice,
Seal'd — by signs the chosen know,
Bought — by love and life the price,
Bless'd — the mighty debt to owe.

"Holy Pilgrim! what for thee
In a world like this remain?
From thy guarded breast shall flee,
Fear and shame, and doubt and pain.
Fear — the hope of Heaven shall fly,
Shame — from glory's view retire,
Doubt — in certain rapture die,
Pain — in endless bliss expire."

I will now say a word on the two last series of poems, which were published in Mr. Crabbe's own lifetime. I mean "The Tales," and "The Tales of the Hall." "The Tales" are narrative dramas from familiar life, and the most powerful of them are those in which the author, true to his genius, confines himself to tragic subjects, in which he deals with the guilt and sorrow of humanity. On these subjects, the author is always potent; the very sources of the passions are open to him; he touches the hard rock in the wilderness of calamity, and at his touch, it gushes out from its deepest fountains. When he writes on topics of sadness, his pen is not merely dipped in tears, but in tears that lie in the innermost cavities of the heart.

These general remarks apply with equal truth to the "Tales of the Hall," for they are similar in spirit to the "Tales," except only, that occasionally they soar into aristocratic life, losing force as they aspire, and that they have a slender thread of connection. The connection is merely this: Two brothers meet after long separation and various fortunes; the elder rich, a bachelor, and retired to his native village; the younger, a wanderer, a man of family, and poor. The poor brother comes by invitation of the rich; during the visit both tell stories, and these stories are "The Tales of the Hall." The brothers, though of opposite characters, please each other exceedingly, and on parting, the poor man finds that his richer relative has made him independent for life.

Let me give a brief illustration from each of these series of "The Tales." The Patron is one of the most affecting; full of meaning and full of feeling. It is this tale which Sir Walter Scott would have his children get by heart. The son of a humble man is gifted by Heaven with genius. He writes verses and is applauded. He goes to college, and is distinguished.

He becomes ambitious, and dreams as youthful poets dream —

"Fame shall be mine, then wealth shall I possess,
And beauty next an ardent lover bless;
For me the maid shall leave her nobler state,
Happy to raise and share her poet's fate."

The bard ingratiates a young lord by some satiric squibs, which gain the young lord an election for the borough; the bard in turn gains an invitation to his lordship's country mansion. The father's letter to him while there, is a masterpiece of sterling sense, and affectionate eloquence. Mark the shrewd insight of one paragraph: —

"Prudence, my boy, forbids thee to commend
The cause or party of thy noble friend;
What are his praises worth, who must be known
To take a patron's maxims for his own?
When ladies sing or in thy presence play,
Do not, dear John, in rapture melt away;
'T is not thy part, there will be list'ners round,
To cry *divine!* and dote upon the sound:
Remember, too, that though the poor have ears,
They take not in the music of the spheres:
They must not feel the warble and the thrill,
Or be dissolved in ecstasy at will:
Besides, 't is freedom in a youth like thee
To drop his awe and deal in ecstasy."

The father was old, the son was young; the father was a homely man, the son was a poet; and how could the young poet understand the old and homely man? and what is it of joy or hope that a young poet cannot believe? The lord had a sister, she was beautiful as heaven and as kind. The poet, as a matter of course, loved her, and she was not displeased. He thought of no obstacle; how could there be? He who had climbed Parnassus, and stolen fire from the skies, why should he not reach a damsel's heart, though that heart was amidst the peerage? Our poet wrapped himself in his delirious enchantment; alas, that the charm should too soon be broken! He forgot that ladies out of London soon find trees and fields but dull concerns, and are grateful to any animal which relieves the monotony; he forgot that fashionable ladies will sometimes weary of parrots and poodles, and take even a poet as a substitute; and in this ignorance, the unhappy wretch misunderstood the raptures of the high-born maiden, who listened to his song and seemed delighted all the while. The day of departure arrives; the carriage is at the door; —

"The ladies came; and John in terror threw
One painful glance, and then his eyes withdrew;
Not with such speed, but he in other eyes
With anguish read, 'I pity, but despise.

Unhappy boy! presumptuous scribbler! you
To dream such dreams! be sober, and adieu.'
"Then came the noble friend — 'And will my lord
Vouchsafe no comfort? drop no soothing word?
Yes, he must speak.' He speaks, 'My good young friend,
You know my views; upon my care depend;
My hearty thanks to your good father pay,
And be a student. Harry, drive away.'"

The miserable dupe goes to London, and cannot even see his lordship. After dangling in his ante-room, time after time, in all the anguish of suspense, instead of promotion in the church, he receives, by the hand of a menial, a commission for a low excise clerkship. He tries to fulfil its duties, but breaks down under the weight of despair, and is found near his home, whither he had rambled in haggard madness. He recovers his reason, and dies calmly among his lamenting relations.

"Meantime the news through various channels spread,
The youth once favor'd with such praise, was dead.
'Emma,' the lady cried, 'my words attend,
Your siren smiles have kill'd your humble friend:
The hope you raised can now delude no more,
Nor charms, that once inspired, can now restore.'
Faint was the flush of anger and of shame
That o'er the cheek of conscious beauty came:
'You censure not,' said she, 'the sun's bright rays,
When fools imprudent dare the dangerous gaze;

And should a stripling look till he were blind,
You would not justly call the light unkind:
But is he dead? and am I to suppose
The power of poison in such looks as those?'
She spoke, and, pointing to the mirror, cast
A pleased, gay glance, and court'sied as she past.
"My lord, to whom the poet's fate was told,
Was much affected, for a man so cold;
'Dead!' said his lordship, 'run distracted, mad!
Upon my soul, I'm sorry for the lad;
And now, no doubt, th' obliging world will say
That my harsh usage help'd him on his way:
What! I suppose, I should have nurs'd his muse,
And with champagne have brighten'd up his views;
Then had he made me famed my whole life long,
And stunn'd my ears with gratitude and song.
Still should the father hear that I regret
Our joint misfortune — yes! I'll not forget.'"

"The Lover's Journey" is one of those gayer fancies by which Crabbe but too seldom relieves the gloom of his darker descriptions; and yet, not less in this than in his deepest musings, does he show himself the subtle analyst of inward feelings, the accurate observer of outward objects. The story is exceedingly simple. A young man upon a summer's day mounts his horse to visit, at a few miles distance, the lady of his love His mind is elated with rejoicing thoughts, wrapt in gladsome expectation; every thing he sees is bright and fair, all that he hears is music. In the first part of his journey he passes through heat and dust, over unsheltered moss and moor, but instead of crying "all is barren," he finds that all is beautiful. Arriving at the residence of his mistress, instead of herself, there is a message, that she has gone some miles to visit a friend, and asking him to follow her. Chagrined and disappointed he sets out again, and then, though his way lies amidst the loveliest landscapes, he can see nothing to admire. At last he meets her, and then returning home with her, he takes no notice whatever of external objects, for his mind is too full of internal satisfaction, to be excited at all through the senses. The painting in this poem, and the philosophy, is each in its way admirable. Observe what charms our lover can discern in a bog during his first experience.

"'Various as beauteous, Naturè, is thy face,'
Exclaim'd Orlando: 'all that grows has grace,
All are appropriate; bog, and marsh, and fen,
Are only poor to undiscerning men;
Here may the nice and curious eye explore
How Nature's hand adorns the rushy moor;
Here the rare moss in secret shade is found,
Here the sweet myrtle of the shaking ground;

Beauties are these that from the view retire,
But well repay th' attention they require;
For these my Laura will her home forsake,
And all the pleasures they afford partake.' "

Note what eye-sores he discovers in the fairest and richest scenes during the course of his second experience.

"Forth rode Orlando by a river's side,
Inland and winding, smooth, and full, and wide,
That roll'd majestic on, in one soft flowing tide;
The bottom gravel, flowery were the banks,
Tall willows, waving in their broken ranks,
The road, now near, now distant, winding led
By lovely meadows which the waters fed;
He passed the wayside inn, the village spire,
Nor stopp'd to gaze, to question or admire;
On either side the rural mansions stood,
With hedge-row trees, and hills high-crown'd with wood,
And many a devious stream that reach'd the nobler flood.
" 'I hate these scenes,' Orlando angry cried,
'And these proud farmers! yes, I hate their pride:
See! that sleek fellow, how he strides along,
Strong as an ox, and ignorant as strong;
Can yon close crops a single eye detain
But his who counts the profits of the grain?
And these vile beans with deleterious smell,
Where is their beauty? Can a mortal tell?

These deep fat meadows I detest; it shocks
One's feelings there to see the grazing ox;
For slaughter fatted, as a lady's smile
Rejoices man, and means his death the while.
Lo! now the sons of labor! every day
Employ'd in toil, and vex'd in every way;
Theirs is but mirth assum'd, and they conceal,
In their affected joys, the ills they feel;
I hate these long green lanes; there 's nothing seen
In this vile country but eternal green;
Woods! waters! meadows! will they never end?
'T is a vile prospect. Gone to see a friend!'"

The story of the sisters from the "Tales of the Hall," is told with peculiar tenderness; a softened pathos marks the incidents, and a lyric melancholy pervades the language. Two sisters, of contrasted characters, are attached with an affection rendered stronger by this opposition of tempers. The one is an enthusiastic dreamer, the other a meek and simple spirit. They are orphans. Each has a lover, and each believes her own as constant as the sun. Robbed by a scheming banker of their humble patrimony, they are deserted by their swains. Reduced from competence to poverty, they have nothing to sustain them but hard work and pious resignation. The gentler maiden bears the storm in the strength of meekness, but the poor enthusiast falls under the wreck of her hopes. Her reason fails, and thus, while waiting for death, she raves most eloquent music.

"Let me not have this gloomy view
  About my room, around my bed;
But morning roses wet with dew,
  To cool my burning brows instead.
As flowers that once in Eden grew,
  Let them their fragrant spirit shed;
And every day the sweets renew,
  Till I, a fading flower, am dead.

"Oh, let the herbs I loved to rear
  Give to my sense their perfum'd breath;
Let them be placed above my bier,
  And grace the gloomy house of death.
I'll have my grave beneath a hill,
  Where only Lucy's self shall know;
Where runs the pure, pellucid rill,
  Upon the gravelly bed below:

"There violets on the borders blow,
  And insects their soft light display;
Till, as the morning sunbeams glow,
  The cold phosphoric fires decay.

"That is the grave to Lucy shown,
  The soil a pure and silver sand,
The green, cold moss, above it grown,
  Unpluck'd by all but maiden-hand:

In virgin-earth, till then unturned,
  There let my maiden form be laid;
Nor let my changed clay be spurned,
  Nor for new guest that bed be made.

" There will the lark, the lamb in sport
  In air, on earth, securely play;
And Lucy to my grave resort,
  As innocent, but not so gay.
I will not have the churchyard ground,
  With bones all black and ugly grown,
To press my shivering body round,
  Or, on my wasted limbs, be thrown.

. . . .

" Say not it is beneath my care;
  I cannot these cold truths allow:
These thoughts may not afflict me there,
  But, oh! they vex and tease me now.
Raise not a turf, nor set a stone,
  That man a maiden's grave may trace;
But thou, my Lucy, come alone,
  And let affection find the place."

Our theme has been serious, but not, I trust, unpleasant. We have discoursed of the human heart and the human life. How mighty is this human heart, with all its complicated energies; this living source of all that moves the world! Who would not have it? Who would not have it, even despite of its wanderings and mistakes; with all its sins, its sorrows, and its wrongs. Yes, who would not have it still; with its grief as well as ecstasy, its anguish as well as exultation? Who would not have this full and mighty human heart, this treasury of noble impulses, so aspiring, so sublime! this temple of liberty, this kingdom of heaven, this altar of God, this throne of goodness, so beautiful in holiness, so generous in love! Who would not have it in freedom, ay, in the delirium of freedom, rather than in the slavery of an iron necessity, or the apathy of a stupid instinct? How mysterious is this human life, with all its diversities of contrast and compensation; this web of chequered destinies, this sphere of manifold allotment, where man lives in his greatness and grossness, a little lower than the angels, a little higher than the brutes; where death walks hand in hand with life, and sin with sanctity, and agony with delight; where the procession of the burial mingles with that of the bridal, and the graspings of despair pierce through the wild choruses of revelry; where the castle overlooks the hut, and the palace fronts the prison; and the throne is raised over the hollow of the dungeon; and one man commands a world, and another pines away existence within the circumference of his chain; yet where all have substantial pleasures, and substantial pains, which no condition can entirely destroy, pleasures which the most wretched cannot lose, pains which the most favored must endure. We have in this imperfect scene but a fragment of our story; its opening is here, its issues are in eternity; the hour approaches when the secrets of every heart shall be opened, and the mystery of every life be made known; till then, the wisdom of the heart is faith, and the majesty of the life is virtue.

THE MORAL PHILOSOPHY

OF

BYRON'S LIFE.

To select for a popular discourse, a topic on which so much has been written, and written finely, may seem an undertaking of considerable presumption. But a theme so full of moral import is not readily exhausted; and an individual impression, however humble, may not, even on this subject, be without its value and its place. And now that the spell of the poet's presence does not enthrall us, we are in a position to form an impartial opinion, and we may dare to express it. This was scarcely the case before. Prejudices in favor of Byron or against him, with which we have no concern, operated on his contemporaries; and the enthusiasm which, while his thrilling tones were fresh in men's hearing, blunted the moral sense and silenced the moral judgment, has long become sobered. Admired for the splendor of his genius, and feared for its power, the stammer of his censors was unnoted in a tempest of applause ; his vices were lost in the lustre of his fame, and his morbid passions secured a morbid sympathy. The fervor which his poetry then inspired, compelled multitudes to think lightly of his sins ; now, that multitudes, in their coldness, revert to his transgressions, the reaction seems to turn against his poetry. Both the moral and the critical antithesis, in each case, has an element of error. I shall try to give my own convictions with simplicity. I have arrived at them through no unfriendly prepossessions ; and if my tendency would lead me in any degree from strictness, it would be much to extenuate, but naught set down in malice.

For order, though not for information, it will be needful to trace a rapid outline of the life, which forms a text for the reflections that follow.

Byron was born in London in 1788, and with some faint prospect of a peerage. His father's profligacy had left him but small means of a gentlemanly competence. His childhood was spent in the north of Scotland, where his wayward mother supported herself and him in economical decency. Opportunely for Byron, the heir who stood between him and fortune died, and a coronet fell upon his boyish head. Byron was not insensible to the distinction. The morning after his recognition as a lord, when his name in the class received the addition of "*dominus*," unable to reply "*adsum*," he burst into tears. Even in boyhood, Byron never forgot his rank, and there were occasions when he did not remember it with the kindest grace. His reply to his teacher, Dr. Butler, in refusing, out of pique, his invitation to dinner, is an instance of haughty discourtesy. His refusal and reason are equal in rudeness. He coolly rejected the request; and when it was inquired why? "Because, Dr. Butler, if you should happen to come into my neighborhood, when I was staying at Newstead, I certainly should not ask you to dine with me, and therefore I feel that I ought not to dine with *you*." Nor is this aristocratic temper, less apparent in other youthful moods, or more gracious. Addressing lines to a humble favorite of his own age, he shows the consciousness of their respective ranks in the opening words:

"Let folly smile to view the names
Of thee and me in friendship joined."

Thus marking a distinction which a boy of spontaneous and simple character would scarcely have thought about, and to whom it would have presented no occasion for the smiles of folly or of wisdom.

Later in life Byron would know that there was no real friendship in this juvenile companionship. Such condescension and concession, with such direct announcement of condescension and concession, have no accordance with genuine friendship. Friendship, like love, is self-forgetful. The only inequality it knows is one that exalts the object, and humbles self. The object is so thoroughly precious, so enriched to the imagination, and so endeared to the heart, that, in its supreme worth, all else is forgotten, and all else is lost. It may be doubted whether Byron, throughout his life, ever had for any of his own sex such friendship, or for any of the other ever had such love. One friend he confesses to have had, but that one was not of the human family. This friend was his dog Boatswain, to whose remains he gave a monument.

> " To mark a friend's remains, these stones arise;
> I never knew but one, and here he lies."

If this is a poetical exaggeration, the cynicism of impassioned youth, the confession of his maturity in sober prose, does not fall far short of it. As to friendship, he says " it is a propensity in which my genius is very limited. I do not know the male human being, except Lord Clare, the friend of my infancy, for whom I feel any thing that deserves the name ; all my others are men-of-the-world friendships. I did not even feel it for Shelley, however much I admired and esteemed him; so that not even vanity could bribe me into it; for of all men, Shelley thought highest of my talents, and perhaps of my disposition."

The school-boy days of Byron were lonely and unprotected. Without guardianship or control, he was thrown upon his own impulses; and if these impulses were brave and generous, they were also wild and reckless. A melancholy reflection is that, with which he refers to the commencement of his college life. "From that moment," he says, "I began to grow old in my own esteem, and in my esteem age is not estimable. I took my gradation in the vices with great promptitude; but they were not to my taste, for my early passions, though violent in the extreme, were concentrative, and hated division and spreading abroad. I could have left or lost the whole world with or for that which I loved; but, though my temperament was naturally burning, I could not share in the commonplace libertinism of the place and time without disgust. And yet this very disgust, and my heart thrown back upon itself, threw me into excesses perhaps more fatal than those from which I shrank."

Byron came forth from college with no lofty scholarship, but with a world of undeveloped genius. He then commenced his manhood's life in literary combat and pecuniary embarrassment. His volume of "Juvenile

Sentimentalism" was baptized by the Edinburgh Review in those waters of bitterness, which were never intended for the literary salvation of the bantlings on which they were poured. If the feeble offspring shivered under the ablution, the youthful father did not share its weakness. In plain words, he chastised his chastisers; but the strokes which they gave "with whips, he returned with scorpions." To the battle of criticism, he joined the perplexities of excess. Byron's fortune, small at any time for his station, was nothing for his desires. Newstead beheld a new order of brotherhood, in which sensual orgies took the place of spiritual vespers; in which bacchanalian chants answered to religious psalmody; in which young rakes, garmented as old monks, crowned the mysteries of debauch by quaffing Burgundy from a human skull. The soul which seeks all its revenue of pleasure from the senses, quickly leaves them bankrupt; and senses taxed as Byron taxed them, were not long in reaching pauperism. Satiated and disgusted, he then turned to travel for change of scene and change of passion. In the sunny lands of Spain and Greece he found wherewith to feed his restless cravings, to meet his longings for intense emotion, and to gratify his wishes for the wild and the beautiful. Greece especially, with its fair skies, its ideal past, and its broken present; its majesty in fragments, but in fragments that reflected lingering beams of its primitive splendor; Greece, thus dishevelled but lovely in her rags, was congenial, in all respects, to his musing and despondent thoughts.

Returned from this vagrant tour to his native land, he had scarcely a friend to meet him on its shores. His mother, whom habit, notwithstanding her coarseness and caprice, had rendered dear to him, had died soon after his arrival. "At three and twenty," he says, "I am left alone, and what more can I be at seventy? It is true, I am young enough to begin again; but with whom can I retrace the laughing part of life?" Alas that three and twenty, a gifted man, should feel that he had past the laughing part of life! But from this his first exile he brought "Hints from Horace," which may count as nothing, and two cantos of the magnificent "Childe Harold," which count for precious treasure. Two or three days before the publication of Childe Harold, he spoke for the first time in the House of Lords, and was proud of his success. His speech evinced a love of liberty and a sympathy for the poor, but it was defective in political knowledge, and wanted the range and depth of a masterly production. Childe Harold appeared, and the twinkle of his maiden declamation was lost in the blaze of its glory. "I awoke one morning," he says, "and found myself famous." From that morning his destiny was revealed; and his destiny was poetry.

Byron burst rapidly, not only into glory, but into fashion. Still, he was in extremity. He wanted position, and he wanted money. His friends advised him to marry, and marriage of the right sort, they said, would insure him both. But whom was he to marry? "Miss Milbanks," says the bard. "By no means," objects his confidant; "Miss Milbanks would not suit him. She was a learned lady, and at the time had no fortune." The confidant, meanwhile, writes a proposal to another lady. The proposal is refused. "You see," says Byron, "Miss Milbanks is the person. I will write to her." The loving epistle was written; the objecting friend was softened in perusing it. "Well, really," quoth the friend, "it is a very pretty letter; it is a pity it should not go. I never read a prettier one." "Then it shall go," said Lord Byron. So it did go, and Miss Milbanks consented to become Lady Byron. Then came the poet's murmuring at the bustle which the nuptials must occasion, and at the annoyance of wearing a blue coat when he preferred a black one. Anxious about many things, he forgot his bride, even at the altar, and when the ceremony was over, addressed her as Miss Milbanks.

Love there was not on either side; but there was

something worse than the want of it on Byron's. If passion and eccentricity excuse many of his errors, this error has no such apology. It was an act of deliberate coolness, an act of remorseless indifference, in which the happiness of a human heart was staked upon chance, and jeopardized with banter. The rejected of one offer, Byron yet made another, and, if we are to believe his own avowal, this repeated offer arose out of no change from his original sentiments. It was made, too, in a spirit reckless of consequences, that must fall heaviest, if evil, on the weaker party, in a spirit of burlesque and levity, that seemed alike devoid of tenderness and respect.

The separation, therefore, of Lord and Lady Byron was no mysterious matter, notwithstanding all that has been said about its mystery. It was a very simple and a very obvious consequence of such a union; a result in perfect accordance with the laws of human nature, however concealed may lie the preliminary incidents. Lord Byron was subjected to no common odium, on the one hand; on the other, he was indemnified by no common sympathy. That the poet deeply suffered, we must believe, if we credit not his words alone, but his mere humanity. That the lady had her anguish, too, we can as little doubt; but the poet could give his sorrow charmed sounds, that strongly moved the world from blame to pity. The lady chose the course which dignity and her sex defined, retirement and silence.

The poet, it has been said, was enthusiastic and ardent; the lady, orderly and cold. The merits or the faults of either cannot be apportioned here, nor the dispute of his or her defenders settled, in reference to the separation ; but, subsequent to that event, impartial judges would, I think, award the lady the praise of heroism as well as the praise of virtue. The widow, made already in the youthful wife, concealed her tears and suppressed her sighs; the maiden's hopes and the matron's pride blasted in a day, provoked no harsh complaint; and when the household sanctuary, which every woman consecrates with the brightest and choicest dreamings of her heart, became a solitude, it retained its holiness, if it lost its gladness. The poet sought relief in wild excess and bolder power; the lady had chosen a separate path, and in quietness she walked it. But yet, her way of life was not inactive ; many works of mercy had her care; the poor, and the lowly, and the ignorant, had her sympathy; the sentiments of the good shared her appreciation and communion; the efforts to relieve and raise afflicted man obtained, without request, her blessing and her aid. Poetic fire may dazzle with intenser beams than the light of virtue ; but it is this light that falls benignly on the obscurity of the wretched, which the glow of poetry never warms. It is this light that gilds an immortal's crown, when death turns the fairest bays to dust.

Byron, from the period of disunion, kept no terms with society or with his constitution. His second exile was a moral outlawry. His life at Venice was a prodigality of profligacy. He wallowed to the lips in evil. He cast all sentiment to the winds, and drank the cup of sensualism to the dregs. It has been said that he made his residence a harem, but harem is a term that means propriety itself, compared with Byron's residence at Venice. The portion of his days and nights, not squandered among shameless associates, was devoted to Don Juan. Bewildered, exhausted, dejected, disgusted, he formed at last a union, in which the evil of guilt may have been as great, but the form of it was less vile. The Marquis of Guiccioli lost a wife; Byron gained a companion; and this was regarded by certain of his friends as a happy connection, a most auspicious return to propriety. But life had no more to give him. The pungency of pleasure is transient as the foam that mantles round its brimming cup, but Byron had long since reached the sediment. Power had become habit, applause as vapid as an oft-repeated tune; fame and glory could charm no more, for the heart was cold, and the ear was dull. Ambition was lost in familiar sway; desire was reft of zest or freshness; love, in its triumph or its sadness, in expectance or dependence, was extinct; in this prostrate apathy, in this drear and bleak satiety, one source of excitement more remained in arms, in arms directed against oppression in the cause of the patriotic brave. In this impulse he turned his face again to Greece; but it was too late for trophies or for fight, and Greece gave him a deathbed.

Already in the prime of years, when the mighty strain of his coral song was vibrating through the world, already the garden of life had become a desert, without a flower and without a stream; the sun had passed from his sky, scarcely was a star in the gloomy void of being; exiled and alone, amidst savage clamor and foreign hordes, he closed his course on earth in grief and darkness. "Poor Greece," he murmured, "poor town, my poor servants! Why was I not aware of this sooner! My hour is come! I do not care for death, but why did I not go home, before I came here? There are things which make the world dear to me; for the rest, I am content to die!" On the evening of April 18, 1824, Byron said, I shall now go to sleep; he turned round, and slumbered soundly; once again on the next day he opened his eyes, immediately he closed them; the physician felt his pulse, it had ceased to beat for ever.

All was silent in that palace lately so royally tenanted; "the chambers of imagery" were empty; the music in its halls was still; its harps were broken, and its bells had thrown their last vibration upon the winds of time. How true is human nature at last to all its instincts, and to all its affections. In the solemn hour which delivers the soul from illusive vanities to its primitive emotions, Byron cast away his petulance and his scorn; and Byron, as the humblest of his species, clung to simple feelings and native memories. Where he was born, there he would die; where he had his home, there he would find his grave.

Many and impressive are the aspects of this eventful history: each mind according to its peculiar associations, will have its own mode of viewing it. I shall select but two obvious positions, as simple in statement as they are evident in fact. Byron, with most rare endowments, was wretched: this is one. Byron, with great moral delinquency, was an object of peculiar interest: this is the other. In considering these two positions, with their causes and connections, the moral philosophy of Byron's life, as I apprehend it, will appear in natural and progressive development.

Byron, with most rare endowments, was wretched.

I assume this as an admitted fact. Let us then proceed to examine and analyze its import.

A radical evil in Byron's life was the absorbing consciousness of self. Existence can never appear in its true relations considered from the point of self; nor can the actions or events that make the sum of existence, be from this point rightly interpreted, or rightly directed. A life, therefore, in which self is an absorbing principle, is a confusion, a thing of mistakes and dislocations, wrong respecting itself and all that surrounds it, its position is continually that of strife, and its experience that of disappointment. No soul, however grand, can be a centre for the motions of God's spiritual universe, or a final cause for the adjustments of his providence. Any of us has but an atom's place in that immensity of individualities for which, as for our own, God's universe is constructed, and God's providence is arranged. Living out of ourselves as well as in, we can discern marvellous adaptation in this boundless system of contrasts, and we can rejoice in the harmony which we discern. Considering, however, this system as it will often press upon ourselves, and only in reference to ourselves, we give to a single element an importance that is infinitely disproportioned; the whole then seems wrong, and we are unhappy. When to a mistake so fatal, we add inordinate desires and an active imagination, our being is not merely discord, but rebellion; rebellion against the wisdom and the might of Heaven. Deceived in the notion of our strength, we are defeated, but not humbled; incapable of the magnanimous virtues of content and patience, we invoke around us the demons of misanthropy and disbelief. It is not that our expectations are such as must most often be reversed, the temper also of soul is such as can least endure their reversal. "O, you are sick of self, Malvolio," saith Olivia, "and taste with a distempered appetite. To be generous, guiltless, and of a free disposition, is to take things for bird-bolts, that you deem cannon balls." So wrote Shakspeare, the sage and seer of the human heart.

If with this consciousness of self, as agents, we have as strong a consciousness of others as observers, we are doubly sensitive; and these two tendencies usually go together. When self has been a frequent object of our own consciousness, the habit of attention gives to the existence it implies, an importance corresponding to our force of realization; and that so important in our own esteem, we cannot suppose wholly indifferent in the esteem of others. If such is not a consciousness, it is a desire or a fear, a desire for a praise or a fear of censure. Persons of strong self-consciousness are those who write journals and autobiographies; and journals and autobiographies are the fruits of two energetic feelings; first, of the individual being, secondly, the desire to reveal it, including the inference, of course, that it is worth revealing. The mental temperament here specified is entirely irrespective of the actual excellence or insignificance of the matters themselves. Whatever be the difference of their intrinsic value, the essence of the character is the same. It is of no account what volume — whether a world or a village — the capacity occupies, what space the interest can fill; radically, the elements of character are identical which find expression in the confessions of an Augustine, or the experiences of a rustic devotee. Those who are much engaged with their own sensation, complacently imagine that all society is concerned about them; and the delusion pertains to dunces, as well as to men of genius. Rousseau pondered his own ideas until being was agony, and mankind appeared to his tormented fancy in conspiracy to destroy him. Vainly was the world busy with affairs far opposite to his; the world to him was in the direction of his own contemplation, and that was inward upon his trembling heart. Dennis, the critic, distant enough from Rousseau, was disrespectful to France in a stupid play; he implored the Duke of Marlborough to have his name included in the treaty of peace which that nobleman was negotiating, to shield his criticship from the vengeance of the offended French.

Few men were ever more under this double influence than Lord Bryon; an influence to all the nobler moral energies, most blighting and most deadly. Alive to his own inward existence, even to agony, he was exquisitively sensitive that this existence should make impression in the world. He would be a cynic, but his austerity should be known; he could soliloquize on misery, but he would have an audience to hear him. Casting himself recklessly against the world's proprieties, no one writhed more under censure, not the censure of the great moral instinct of society, but of mere conventionalism — the conventionalism, too, of the smallest cliques, which he so fiercely denounced, and which he seemed so to despise. Thus, from two sources, he was the subject of constant excruciation; from self and from society; from morbid contemplation of the one, from disjointed relations with the other; provoking its odium, and writhing under, while he seemed to scorn it; scouting its sanctions, yet angry and indignant when the violation reacted in torture. The inward and the outward conditions of Byron's life were those of unrest, that knew not peace; remote from harmony, and therefore, from happiness.

The character of Byron was lamentably defective in

single-mindedness, a quality essential to life's happiness, and equally essential to life's moral beauty. Lord Byron never leaves upon us the impression of an unconscious simplicity. We do not think of him with a cordial familiarity, as we do of Shakspeare, whom yet we enshrine in such heart-consenting reverence. We stand away from Byron, not as we would with awe in the presence of a godly nature, but as we would in fear of etiquette on a first introduction to a monarch in official robes. Something artificial adheres to Byron in all he does, and from habit it adheres to him when his intentions are most sincere. Mrs. Siddons could not ask for beer but in a manner that startled the butler ; Byron could scarcely swim or ride, but the observation of mankind was before him. Desiring to be an object of attention, — and large must have been his measure, if he had not as much attention as he desired, — Byron saw the world as a stage, and conformed his gestures and his attitudes to the requirements of the scene. Doubtless, beneath the tinsel and the spangles, there was much that was genuine and hearty. A man of fewer impulses than Lord Byron had from nature, could not always keep in the theatre and wear its costume, and a man of fewer social sympathies would need a circle of ease and confidence. But even in these, Byron understood the force of dramatic contrast, and from the clashing of the near impression with the distant, could heighten the effect of both. A graceful amiability of which his manner was, when he chose, peculiarly susceptible, was a miracle of light to those, who formed their idea of him in the Corsair or in Cain; but, a freedom which did not suit his humor, he could at once repel.

The want of single-mindedness is seen in manifold affectation. If we credit certain of Byron's critics and biographers, Byron often assumed an air of mystery, that something awful might be supposed behind,—"a deed without a name." Except he intended to make merry with his dupes, the vanity was a wretched one; and, if he hoped his deception to be successful, he must have ranked them by the standard of nursery superstitions. But, there is no need in this or other cases, that might be mentioned, to resort to doubtful accusation; instances enough are plain, which, though not criminal, are characteristic. He began his course in affecting to despise money, and he ended in affecting to love it. At first he pretended to disdain remuneration for his works, but subsequently his publisher found him an exacting author. This is not the only inconsistency which we observe in him with respect to his compositions. With the sternness of a literary Brutus, he seems at times to give up his intellectual offspring to the death-sentence of criticism ; a literary Brutus, however, has this advantage over the old Roman, that the life of his darling may be snug in another copy ; and so it was with Byron's. Shelley had given judgment against "The Deformed Transformed ;" Byron, in the presence of Shelley and other witnesses, consigned the manuscript to the flames, with the tranquillity of an inquisitor burning a heretic ; but a short while after, the drama appeared in its unmaimed integrity. He assumed, on occasions, a supreme indifference for his writings, "I don't care," he says, "two lumps of sugar for my poetry, but for my costume and correctness, on these points I will combat lustily." Literary affectation he carried to a degree of caprice, which no man would have dared, but one who had his amazing popularity. And here, also, we have the theatrical tendencies of his character ; for some instances of whims, mark his conduct with respect to his works, which would better suit a petted opera singer, than a mighty poet. He corresponded at one time with Murray, to repurchase and recall his copyrights ; he even refunded money he had just received. Murray doubted the seriousness of the whole matter ; and from the ease with which Byron was dissuaded, we may doubt it also. Enough has now been said on this topic of affectation.

Let us turn to another source in Byron's character of suffering and of wrong. It was his immense inward energy, broken into wild and unchastened impulse. This energy, which had needed the wisest discipline, was from the first left to the promptings of its own blind will. This energy, which had called for a system of rigorous moral culture, was subjected to no restraint of custom, and to no check of law. This energy, which, rightly ordered, would have been a beauty and a light in the dwelling-place of life, shattered and confused, only filled it with turbulence and with disaster. This energy, expressed in permanent affections, and directed by great principles, would have made genius as the creativeness of God, a holy power of love and wisdom; but Byron had neither permanent affections nor great principles, and his genius, therefore, became an instrument of pain to himself; to others, a prophecy of evil, or a voice of denial. Byron had no permanent affections; to keep to literal truth, he had few. Those of kindred, which are often the only earthly compensation of poverty, which last through change and travel, and in exile and in death, bring back the beat of childhood's being to the failing pulse, and the bliss of childhood memories to the parting spirit, — those were not for Byron; they hovered not around his titled youth, to guide his steps; they came not up in the recollections of his vagrant existence, in guardian fancies to keep his heart.

Neither was his the blessing of a pure and exalted love, to be a lamp of ideal beauty and disinterested hope amidst the clouds and quagmires of the passions. The boyish feelings which idolized Miss Chaworth might have ripened into devoted and confirmed sentiment; as it was, they were rejected, and that fine strung ear, which longed to catch the name of Byron syllabled in the softness of a maiden's reverie, heard it uttered only in derision of his lameness: "Do you think I could like that lame boy?" A charm was dissolved by these words, harmlessly spoken in a girl's indifference; words that fell without intention, as sparks upon a hidden mine, and left a rent of blackness which time could never close. This void seems always to have remained unoccupied; a thin surface may, indeed, have overspread it. On such foundation, and above such emptiness, Byron raised his domestic altar; it required but a breath to shake it; the breath was not wanting, and it fell, never to be rebuilt.

It is our *inward* world that makes our outward; the life that we see is but the reflection of the one which we feel, for which heaven, earth, society are mirrors, and the thoughts and associations of the soul the archetypes and objects. The inward world of Byron soon became a chaos, and therefore the outward world in his native locality became disorganized. All that renders the native soil endeared to fancy was blasted in his morbid life. The feelings which consecrate the spot that nursed us, which are the music of its airs and the beauty of its skies, the glory of its grass and the splendor of its flowers ; these feelings were not crushed in Byron, but they were empoisoned, and therefore his country is ever in his imagination, not a blessed reminiscence, but a troubled dream. If all these primitive emotions in Byron were so despoiled, it is not wonderful that secondary ones should share their injury. If Byron had but discomfort in those sacred places of the breast where the choicest guests are sheltered, we could expect but chill and ruin in the outer courts. When kindred and country, and love and friendship are dead, we are dead. Human affections are so entwined with each other, that the chord of one can seldom be untuned, that the harmonies of all are not disturbed. Sad, then, must be the discord, when it is not one but many that are dissonant. Byron's sister and daughter were dear, and cherished sacredly in all his evil ; which intimate that he was made for better courses than those wherein he walked.

Permanent affections Byron had not, but flashings of kindliness constantly evince that a good spirit struggled with the evil, and had his moments of victory. References to early days, yearnings over departed friends, sad dreamings of broken hopes, glowing tributes to England, occasional deeds of princely generosity, habitual pity for distress, and sympathy with misfortune, we discover in all the stages of his progress. Still, unsettled and unsatisfied, his energy was in no direction to bring the soul to calm fruition, yet energy must, in some direction, come to its limit; thence his rushing into all excess of passion.

The passions are at once tempters and chastisers. As tempters, they come with garlands of flowers, on brows of youth; as chastisers, they appear with wreaths of snakes on the forehead of deformity. They are angels of light in their delusion; they are fiends of torment in their inflictions; they mislead only to recriminate, they flatter that they may deride; they show us a false glory but to mock us; they raise us to the cloud-capped pinnacle, to dash us fiercely to the stony ground. Like the daughters of Lear, they first beguile their victim of his sovereignty and power; and when their dupe is enfeebled and dependent, robbed of every friendly support, of every pleasant companion, a beggar in consolation and in hope, they cast him out upon the desert, to the darkness of the night, and the fury of the tempest.

Byron, I have said, was not sustained by great principles. He had no settled philosophy. In metaphysics, he was by turns idealist and materialist; a sceptic and a dogmatist. In literature, his dicta were commonly but whims, the mere assertions of caprice or paradox. He eulogized Kirke White, and yet he disparaged Keats; Pope had his rapture, and even Hayley gained his praise; but Shakspeare won from him no enthusiasm, and the rare mention which he made of this great name, was in coldness or in censure. To contemporary genius, which was *caviare* to the multitude, which had no cheers from popular applause, he never extended fellowship or sympathy; and in some instances, his sin was worse than the simple want of appreciation. Wordsworth he treated with a coarseness and indignity disgraceful and ungenerous; and Southey he pursued with an indefatigable vengeance, which no rancor of the *critic* can justify in the *poet*. The conduct of Shelley to his persecutors is a strong and exalted contrast to that of Byron. In morals, the code of Byron, if such a designation can be applied to mere eccentricities of will and desire, was a mixture of the cynical and the sensual, a combination of Timon and Epicurus. In government, he vibrated between democracy and despotism: power he would have perfect in the many or the one, but not power complicated between the many and the one. "Give me," he says, "a republic or a despotism. A Republic," he exclaims; "look on the history of the earth, Rome, France, Holland, America, for that (eheu!) Commonwealth, and compare it with what they did under masters!" But, however much Byron esteemed liberty, and despised aristocracy, in temper he was an aristocrat; he was *for* the people, but he was not *of* them.

Religion, it will be asserted, he had or had not, according to the view which the critic may take of religion or of Byron. But he is a poor critic both of religion and of character, who does not find at least the elements of religion in Byron, chaotically, it may be, yet sublimely active. Byron had no formal religious training: no mother from his childhood was near, to put a prayer on his lips, to whisper a thought of the good God or of the blessed Jesus to his opening heart, to teach him at her knee to consecrate each morning and night, with innocent and simple worship. He knew nothing of Sunday schools or Scripture lessons, and though a peer of England, a born legislator, and under the guardianship of the country's most venerable educational institutions, the nonage of the most neglected pauper could not be spiritually more desolate. But the religious instinct, which the poetic genius cannot but strongly feel, had, in a wild way, its growth and energy.

It appears early in Byron's self-revealings, and they show it to the last.

Byron's soul was dark, unhoping, not indeed trembling, nor yet believing; but its habitual ponderings were over the deep things of existence, its affinities were with whatever in being is infinite and awful. If he did not discern goodness and justice clearly in the universe, no one than he seems more affected by the limitless Presence in it of Power and Intelligence; and with these, through oceans, stars, mountains, deserts, caverns, volcanoes, cataracts, tempests, he ever held profound communion. Such communings make not a little of his song; a song, when vocal with these, if not filial and trustful, yet not gross, not earthly; a song, then, sad, but never whining; often dirge-like in its music, but always massive, rich, and solemn. Frequently, he looks only at our nature on the side of its littleness, sports with it perversely and cynically; but his true sympathy is with it in its greatness, its strength, its grief, its passions, its mysteries, and its destinies; if he does laugh and sneer, it is only when he comes upon the surface, and you observe by the palpitations of his heart, by the heavings of his breast, and by the nervous quiver of his lip, that he has been diving in deep waters. Having that which rendered him thus susceptible to all that is profound and grand in nature and in man, we wonder not at his appreciation of the most sublime passages in the Bible; and we can easily comprehend the repeated and delighting study, which made him so familiar with the lofty dithyrambics of David and Isaiah, with the fine vehemence of St. Paul, and mystic melody of St. John. Of course I do not say, that Byron was a religious man, as Burns was not; yet both of them had much of the religious nature. Each of them had, with the intensity of his genius, the elements of the religious nature; but neither of them had the principle which combines and shapes these elements into religious character. With the religious character, neither could have lived as he did; without a strong religious nature, Byron could not have written the noblest passages in Childe Harold, nor Burns "The Cottager's Saturday Night."

If Byron, however, has been sinful and unhappy, he has found a biographer who labors with no common devotion to show, that it has been all the better for the world, not because such a life is a beacon, but a glory. Evil and suffering in the soul would seem, according to such critics, not to be hinderances to power, but sinews of strength. But the head must be grievously confused by false reasoning, and the heart deeply imbruted by false morality, before we can believe that a poet has fountains of inspiration in petulance, profligacy, and self-infliction. Byron, with all his transgression, receives injury, both in dignity and manhood, by some reflections of Moore which seem written in a spirit of friendship. A later phase of the poet's life is thus described: "The imaginary or at least retrospective sorrows in which he once loved to indulge, and whose tendency it was, through the medium of his fancy, to soften and refine his heart, were now exchanged for a host of actual, ignoble vexations, which it was even more humiliating than painful to encounter. His misanthropy, instead of being, as heretofore, a vague and abstract feeling, without an object to light upon, and therefore losing its acrimony in diffusion, was now, by the hostility he came in contact with, condensed into individual enmities, and harrowed into personal resentments, and from the lofty, and as it appeared to himself, philosophical luxury of hating mankind in the gross, he was now brought down to the self-humiliating necessity of despising them in detail." The poet's venerable friend, Ali Pacha, himself, would startle at such a passage: "By Mahomet and his beard!" he might well exclaim, "what words are these!" Byron, it seems, is a good boy while no one touches his sugar-plums, but no sooner does any person venture near his dainties, than he kicks and bites with a special fury. The world, by this account, tried him with a hard experience. He was reduced from hating men in the gross, to despising them in detail; and it was only, it would appear, after extreme provocation, that he descended from the ethereality of an abstract misanthropy to the drudgery of a practical contempt. What patience, and what magnanimous forbearance, under such accumulated trials; and what adversity befalls the minstrel's lot, when he must quit the sublime office of detesting his whole species to vent his spleen on Dick and Tom. Seriously, if poetry could end in woe like this, then welcome prose for ever; if this was Byron's state, it was not wretchedness, but perdition.

Byron, with great moral delinquency, was an object of peculiar interest.

Here is the second position, which forms the other topic of these reflections. The truth of this, as of the first, may be simply assumed, for it does not need to be established. No writer ever ingratiated a wider interest than Byron; and this interest was not all of levity or vanity, not merely from love-sick young maidens, and moon-struck young men; pure-souled women implored his salvation in their dying prayers, and religious poets sung of him in connection with the final judgment. If we listened to Byron's own complaints, we should suppose him subjected to the most condign penalties of opinion. But such was not the fact. The popularity of his person and his writings held in England to the last; and the sorrow which followed his ashes to the tomb evinced how many offences a nation can pardon and forget in genius. In Lord Byron's own rank, and in his immediate circle, some may have caused him vexation; but beyond that, what a blaze of fame, and what a pride of triumph! Occasionally, the critical journals administered rebuke; but the same article which condemned his morals, glorified his muse; and Byron must have had a virtuous sensibility, which the world has never been able to discover, if remonstrance against his vice, accompained with homage to his poetry, could very scathingly afflict him. Had their reprobation been louder than it was, success would have stifled their vociferation; and, from the throne of his renown, their agitation seemed but aimless contortion, which could not reach him, and made themselves ridiculous.

Moreover, Byron could have had no faith in their sincerity, no respect for their principles. He knew to what an extent they were venal, factious, heartless; he knew how much they were influenced by malicious and ignoble considerations, by personality, by party, by caste, by every motive except integrity or justice; he daily witnessed good men and noble, set up as objects of their laughter or anathema: little then must he have esteemed the reproofs of those with whom worth, for its own sake, had no sacredness, and genius, discolored by their prejudice, no illumination. What could Byron care for their mocking of counsel, their make-believe of their preachment, their cant of virtue, their twaddle of formalism, when the whole current of their utterance tended only to reveal its hypocrisy, and to sound its hollowness?

What are we then to infer from the popularity of Byron? Are we to conclude from it, the moral degradation of the age, a pervading disorder of the public conscience? I do not think so. Whence, then, are we to seek the cause? Partly, I apprehend, in the power of genius in itself, and more specially in that power as it was modified in Byron; partly in the mitigations which his life presented; mitigations, which came before men's thoughts heightened by all the enchantment which was associated with the poet's name.

To begin with the latter. In alluding to these, I sincerely repel the doctrine, that character is the result of circumstances, a doctrine as degrading as it is pernicious. Absolution from a personal sense of guilt is dearly purchased by a loss of the sense of freedom; the consciousness of indwelling divinity is not worthily exchanged for the impunity of a mechanical necessity. But while the essence of character does not arise from circumstances, circumstances have no small influence upon its manifestation. Human nature, compounded as it is, so bound up by many ties with material life, so dependent on external supports, so contingent, too, on events that lie out of our foresight or control; human nature being thus interwoven with so much that is extrinsic, can never, even when it has most individuality, exert a spiritual liberty, that is complete and unrestrained. In our judgments, therefore, about it in any given position, we must take many obstructions into account; candor will require many allowances, and charity will look for more. What we give to men generally, because of our nature's imperfections, we must not withhold from men of genius; for they are men as others; they share their infirmities; and the spirit which can thus discriminate, ought peculiarly to direct any moral criticism on the life of Byron.

Byron was unfortunate in parentage. His father was a rake and a spendthrift; a man without heart and without principle. His mother was a compound of fondness and caprice; in her fondness she was a fool, in her caprice she was a termagant. The temper of Byron, it is said, even in childhood, was passionate and sullen; a natural inheritance, which moral causes were not wanting to increase. The harsh disposition of his parents, their jarring antipathies, their unloving union, their embittered separation, were germs of evil in his childhood's life. They parted, it is true, while he was almost an infant, but many are the fatal impressions which may lie backward of that boundary of consciousness, over which memory does not pass. Early as separation happened, it could not fail of ill ; it was a sad tradition from his early years, and his mother, unhappily, in the monopoly of guardianship, had likewise the monopoly of unfitness.

A trivial bodily defect became to Byron a serious affliction. The matter in itself was slight, but acting on a morbid sensibility, its vexation was lasting and inveterate. Persons wonder why it should be thus ; but this is the ordinary wonder which springs from the incapacity to understand afflictions which we do not feel. The ill of life can no more be discerned by the senses, than its good ; it is not to be measured by any statutory rule, it cannot be graduated by any external scale. It is relative, and not positive ; determined by the mental and moral organization of its subject, by mysterious workings of fancy and emotion, by inward peculiarities of the individual, which only himself can apprehend, and which he cannot always control. Below the surface of all human calamity, there is ever much which the untouched cannot appreciate ; there is a sting which only the stricken heart can feel; there is a grief with which the stranger does not intermeddle. But speculate as we will, the fact practically connected with our observations, remains unaltered. Byron regarded his lameness with inexpressible distress. Reference to it was torture. The most cruel recollection which clung to the memory of his mother, was an allusion in her anger to his deformity; and in the midst of his splendid fame in London, the mimicry of a wretched woman whom he approached with intentions of compassion, was a blow that stunned him.

Whatever could be pleaded in Byron's favor, mankind were predisposed to hear. He had qualities to which mankind give ample charity. He had youth, high birth, fortune, beauty; and these of themselves are a magic which the world does not austerely resist. He had youth, which captivates the senses; and high birth, which allures imagination; and fortune, which bestows independence; and beauty, which flings over all the radiance of its own fair grace. Upon him, as upon so many, the hard condition was not imposed, of long working and late reward; it was not his fate, to grope on to open light through the chill passages of obscurity and penury. Byron became known to the world while life was in its bloom, while the present hour had pleasure, and the future one had hope. He was not like Dryden, of slow development, losing the admiration which comes with love to twenty, and only gaining that which comes with reverence to forty; the sum of early splendor was on the verdure of his spring-tide; it was not his to wait until heavy mists dissolved, and the beams of a sober evening fell upon searėd and yellow leaves. He had not, as Johnson, to wear out his energies through tedious years, which led to apathy as they led to fame; which delayed success, until desire was dead, and friends removed; until "he was indifferent, and could not enjoy it; until he was solitary, and could not impart it." Yet, withal, he was unhappy, and this was but an additional foundation of interest in him.

His first appearance in the world of letters was one to stir the apathetic, and to attract the amiable; and his progress in that world was such, as did not permit the excitement to decline. A volume of poems, in which good nature was the prominent quality, subjected him to discourtesy and injustice. If his retort did not merit the approbation of the wise, it secured him against the ridicule of the critical. Then followed a series of painful experiences, which had more than dramatic stimulus to a public that looked for novelty, and that looked for impulse. It is true, that many of these experiences were mainly of the imagination; but they were uttered with a personality so concentrative, that readers would not believe them to be poetic feigning, or be deprived of their luxury of sensibility. And, because it was a luxury, the more willing they were to indulge it; it was a matter pleasing to self-love to feel so deeply, not for vulgar want, not for ragged destitution, not for plebeian ignorance, not for the ruin of low-born guilt, but for the sublime woes of a melancholy spirit. A sympathy which is merely a luxury, will always have multitudes to share it; for while it flatters the vanity of sentiment, no demand is made on it for action or for sacrifice. It is true, that of real sufferings, many were of the poet's own creation; many the result of sin; but he threw around them such eloquent fascination, that censure had small chance against his spells; while people blamed they read, and while they read they admired. It is true, that many of these sufferings were cynical; but then, with anti-social discontent, there appeared such writhings of distress; in the seeming scorn of opinion, such anxiety for regard; such sadness in mockery, such visitings of gentle thoughts, in the intervals of gloom; through the very tempest of misanthropy, such sweet, low tones in murmurs for affection, not loud, but deep, — that sympathy was always too strong for anger.

But, that which was the vital cause of the interest

which clung to Byron, I have forborne, yet, to mention. It was this which, for the time at least, heightened every excellence, and softened every defect; which enshrined his image and his name, in the beauty of the ideal. It was genius. Does genius, then, subvert the moral law? Does genius counteract the mighty order of moral retribution? By no means. Why then was Byron so popular and so admired, when a man not more sinful, but ungifted, would have been an object of neglect or odium? Such must indeed be admitted. And true it is, that thousands of minds, virtuous minds, who would have shrunk disgusted from contact with actual vice, could never regard Byron with harsh emotions. Is this from affinity with depravity? I think not. Let us examine the fact in its relations to human nature. Our judgment of abstract character does not, except in decided instances, determine our feelings about men; our judgment is the result of reasoning; our feelings, of association. Individuals are presented to our thoughts in pleasant or disagreeable associations, and these pleasant or disagreeable associations are not always graduated by the abstract moral merit or demerit of the individual. Every person's experience will confirm this. Now, crime in an ordinary man, stands clearly and distinctly before us, and crime, as such, is ever odious; but in a man of genius, it is combined with elements which, though not changing its nature, take from it our attention. I do not deny that herein is danger; but my purpose is to analyze a fact, and not to impress a moral. To secure our interest goes far to secure our verdict; to give us an emotion, is to bribe us to concession; and our gratitude often bestows what our justice would refuse. If we decided logically, this would not be; if we acted with the rigor of impassive intellect, it would not be; but complicated as we are, with many tendencies and many senses, the direction of emotion is not always coincident with the absolute and the right.

Moreover, genius is power; and power that is grandest in the human life, the reflection of the Maker's creative spirit. Power is delightful to us, as a mere object; it magnifies and exalts our souls, for it reveals to them in the achievements of others, the grandeur of their own capacities. Those by whom such convictions are impressed upon us have relations that ennoble them; and though in much we may condemn, we only expel them entirely from respect, when they are faithless or malignant. Genius is before us in the power of all that humanity has accomplished; we mourn over it in the scenes of the mighty dead, and we exult in it amidst the works of the not less mighty living; we find its inscription on the tombs of empires; and feel its ever plastic spirit in the origin and progress of greater empires that replace them. But genius is power, not merely as an object, but as an influence, a power that rules our inward nature, that makes our faculties its instruments, and moves them as it wills. The man of genius is not so much at our mercy as we are at his; he puts our grandest being into action, and lifts us from our ashes to the stars; he breaks the nut-shell to which our own small sphere confined us, and with himself we become fellow-citizens in the free universe of God.

Genius is a power, on the whole, benignant, and to it we feel indebted for a large portion of our most precious enjoyment. To what capacity does it not minister, and what capacity does it not enrich. Let any of us who have had an active and enlarged mental existence, remove from it the treasures and the happiness which genius has communicated, and he will find himself equally poor in pleasure and in thought. What would memory be to us, if those worlds of ideas were extinct with which genius has peopled it? Sweep from men's souls the quaint, the merry, the grave, the gentle, the impassioned population, which Shakspeare and Scott alone have introduced there, and would it not be as if a glorious star with a most living race were torn from eternal sunshine and blotted into nothingness? But memory is only one capacity, and that not the most admirable; add to this, the high discourse of reason; the enraptured dreams of fancy; the incitement of the affections; the aspiration of the moral sentiments; the profound agitation of the passions; and who can count the delights of which he has through this agency been made the recipient, the sorrows of which he has been beguiled, the gladness with which he has been enlivened? By history, he has lived in the region of the past, and questioned the heroic and the wise. Fiction has allured him from drudgery to vision, and in the elysium of the ideal, cheated him for an hour of anxious thoughts or sordid cares. If fiction has given him the pleasures of ideal being, eloquence has aroused him to the action of real concerns; in one he has found the ease of reverie, and in the other the dignity of action. Philosophy has traced for him the soul of things, and within his own found the essence of them all. The perfection of the whole, poetry, has communed with him in charmed word; poetry, the eldest voice of time, the undying melody of the heart; poetry, the language of the spirit, the inward sense of history, of fiction, of eloquence, and of philosophy, united to the harmony of sound; these, all in their several modes, are the utterance of genius.

Genius may be connected with perverted morals,

and may be used for evil; but genius in itself is good, and must be ever lovely. Whoever has it, cannot be wholly in the dark; a light there must be in him; and though the light be broken, it is light from heaven. Genius in itself is good; and in any form of manifestation, good must be its leading attribute. For in what is the manifestation of genius? In truth, in beauty, in grandeur. Genius cannot be divorced from reason and from order. If reason and order must therefore pervade all lasting works of genius, wickedness, of which the principles are falsehood and confusion, can never be their dominant constituents. Fine productions may be connected with moral deformity, but that is not their substance; it is not that which fires our admiration; it is not that which genius animates. And as in the production, so in the author. His genius dignifies his person, and to his genius, and not his crimes, we pay our reverence. But his genius is an essential of his nature; it is associated as such, with our idea of him, and we cannot divest that idea of the attractions which it thus derives. We cannot think of the man of genius, as if he had only sins; for, strive as we may, we must include the nobler parts of his nature in our conception, and these nobler parts will mostly stamp their own likeness on the totality; we cannot cut the man in two, and execrate this part while we adore that. Lord

Byron, especially, will defy such an operation, for his genius is not impersonal; it melted into his entire existence; it was entwined with every fibre of his individuality; and it would be as easy to tear from his heart the whole net-work of veins and arteries, and expect it still to beat, as to dissect with critical scalpel his actual being from his poetical, and leave either of them vitality. The one is the palpitation of the other; every movement of sound has its pulse. His poetry is the chronicle of his soul; and whether from confidence or contempt, he lays it bare to our view, and with a reckless independence, leaves himself to our opinion. If our opinion must be severe, we should not, in forming it, forget that he has deprecated nothing by concealment, and that caution might easily have secured him a better name, though it would not have made him a better man.

THE MORAL SPIRIT

OF

BYRON'S GENIUS.

The main characteristics of Byron's genius, it needs no profound sagacity to discern; they are obvious on the face of his compositions; they are strength of passion and strength of will; coördinated by a keen intellect, aided by a memory, not of ponderous learning, but of instinctive facility, enlivened by a fancy of exhaustless association; these attributes give to Byron his peculiarity and his power. This strength of passion and strength of will are embodied in all his impersonations. Pilgrims or corsairs, brigands or bravoes, outcasts or apostates, whatever be their outward costume or their outward lot, they are all thus distinguished. A certain intensity of consciousness or intensity of action is the law of their poetical existence. A life within there must be, of concentrated feeling or concentrated purpose; a life without there must be, of daring or ambition, of danger which knows but death or triumph. And they must be independent as well as intense; impregnable of soul in right or wrong; in all fortunes masters of their own fate; in defeat they must ask no question; in adversity no pity; in suffering they must make no moan; if their hopes are struck, these hopes must die without complaint, and find a silent burial in the broken heart. The beings that Byron conceived in fiction, and those with whom he sympathized in history, are beings of turbulent, but of isolated souls; beings that struggle and that suffer, but that cannot be subdued; beings with whom life must cease to be a desire, when it ceases to be a tumult. To such purpose is the impassioned confession of the Giaour:

> "My days though few, have passed below
> In much of joy, but more of woe,
> Yet still in hours of love or strife
> I've 'scaped the weariness of life;
> Now leagued with friends, now girt with foes.
> I loathed the languor of repose;
> Now nothing left to love or hate;
> No more with hope or pride elate,
> I'd rather be the thing that crawls
> Most noxious o'er a dungeon's walls,

> Than pass my dull unvarying days
> Condemned to meditate and gaze.
> Yet wakes a wish within my breast
> For rest—but not to feel—'t is rest."

This force of inward life connected with a most happy aptitude of utterance, renders Byron a supreme master of language and description. Of all English poets, he is properly the most eloquent. Diction and thought with Byron are not, as the garment and the body, but as the body and the soul, mutually intermingled and coëxistent, melting each into each, and thus blended, forming an inseparable and a living totality. Words answered to will, and every word was the conductor of an impulse or the mirror of a thought. By his wonderful command over language, Byron combines passion and description in a manner which, if all other claims failed, would entitle him to the praise of a special originality. Creation, in his descriptive passages, seems articulate. The elements seem fraught with human consciousness; and human consciousness seems to assume the might of the elements. The tempest lashes ocean with the resentment of man's anger; and man rushes against his fellow with the fury of the deep. Nor is Byron less powerful in the expression of passion simply. Scorn, hate, contempt, derision, come in a boiling torrent from his heated breast, with a vehemence which will not be impeded, and a rapidity which leaves no time for chill. But sentiments nobler than these came from the heart of Byron to his words. Whose words more than Byron's have hymned with honor the memories of the brave? Whose words more than his have chanted sadder requiems amidst the graves of heroes? Whose words have been hurled with more indignant strength than his, at tyrants within their living walls of hirelings-words, that, like electric fire, glanced along the fetters of the bound, and loosened, if they did not break their chains? Is their eloquence more inspiring, is their eloquence more exciting, than the appeals of Byron to the Greeks? Were there not tones from this youthful and titled Briton, which might almost stir Demosthenes in his grave; and could he have arisen from his ashes, would he not rejoice that Greece, even in her misery, could awaken an enthusiasm kindred to his own?

In calling Byron an eloquent poet, I state no vain distinction. Poetry may not be eloquent, as eloquence may not be poetical; and, indeed, eloquent poetry or poetical eloquence is rarely the highest of its kind. Poetry, as such, may be complete in the imagination, and fulfil its office, when it gratifies the sense of beauty; but eloquence must influence the judgment and act on the passions. Eloquence operates within the circle of realities, treads the solid globe, and mingles in the business and the strifes of men; but the native element of poetry is not in the actual but the ideal. Poetry refines, eloquence must arouse; poetry exalts emotion, eloquence governs conviction. Eloquence is not science, neither is it fancy. It is not logic that enkindles souls; nor is it simply an exhibition of the beautiful, which can do this. No; but a facility which, rapidly as thought, breathes feelings, while they burn, into words. Herein Byron transcended every poet of his time, and herein he is the most eloquent. To feel the difference between purely imaginative poetry and eloquent poetry, we need only read in contrast a passage from Spenser's "Faerie Queene" and a passage from Byron's "Childe Harold."

The genius of Byron exhibits in a striking manner the conflict of the ideal with the limited and the sensual. The result is a tone of dejection. The most common life has an ideal which looks for a satisfaction which the limited and the sensual do not afford. We begin life, however, in hoping for this satisfaction from the sources which never can supply it; and though there is speedy certainty of failure, there is not even a late certainty of wisdom. This delusion, which bewilders humanity in the vain endeavor to fill immortal faculties with perishable objects, is a radical and a destructive mistake. It is a central cause of conflict in the moral world; a central cause of a disorganized vitality, and therefore of many crimes and many sorrows. If the most common men soon reach apathy in the senses, what must it be with men of genius, whose life is so much more aspiring and intense? What must it then have been with Byron, whose life, even among men of genius, was a rapid and absorbing life? The issue is plain in his personal experience; we discern it as clearly in his poetry.

The inveterate self-consciousness which imbues Byron's personal experience, also imbues his poetry, connected, though it is, with unrivalled power and exceeding beauty. Byron saw in human life but the extension and reproduction of his own existence. This being of his was reflected back upon himself from the universe. His own existence being untoward, creation, whether of spirit or of matter, seen through it, appeared shrouded in guilt and sadness. The gaze of Byron was on himself, yet not like the fabled Narcissus, with elated vanity, but with sullen thought. It was not, like Narcissus, on beauty, radiant and gentle, but on beauty sombre and impassioned; it was not a vision from circumscribed and placid waters, it was one of huge and manifold reflection, from the depths of ocean, from the depths of heaven, from fiery clouds, from icy mountains, all repeated and diversified in the kaleidoscope of many-colored passions. The Germans have the story of "A man without a Shadow;" but Byron was a man of a thousand shadows.

This reproduction of Byron's own character in his works, was so natural to him, that he was not aware of it; and hence, I have no doubt that his anger was severe against the critics, who marked it as one of his peculiarities. Such however was the fact, and it hindered him, notwithstanding his splendid genius, from being a great dramatic poet. He did not conceive of passion in its universality, he did not conceive of it as it existed in other minds, separate from his own in character and situation. To understand a passion, he needed personal and direct experience. On the deck of a vessel from Constantinople, he found a dagger; looking at it, he said in an under tone, "I should like to know how a person feels after committing a murder!" "The intense wish to explore the dark passions, thus expressed, united, says Moore, with imagination, at length generated the power." To say nothing of the melo-dramatic affectation implied in the incident, it is not, I apprehend, the way in which the higher imagination would have expressed itself. A creative mind, of the more elevated order, would not have required such individual excitement. Shakspeare, I conceive, would not, and he unfolded all passions; of all passions he most powerfully unfolded the darkest.

The progress of Byron's genius is one that grows in strength, but also one that grows in fierceness; one that, at every stage, leaves happiness and the light more distant in the retrospect. Byron's first eminent effort was a burst of youthful anger. That over, he deepens on from sorrow to scorn. The predominant tone of his poetry, even in its best era, is that of despondency; and whenever, in his subsequent productions, he is most gentle and most human, it is to this tone that he returns. And if existence were indeed as Byron seemed to view it, I see not how any could properly indulge in cheerfulness. If man is a compilation of worthless atoms, struck out by chance or shaped by a Power who despises his own workmanship; if man's life is a mockery, a phantasmagoria of cheats and deceivings; if his youth is a bubble, and his age a blank; if his affections are delusions; his hopes but the visions of a starveling, the seeming paradise which the frenzied and famished mariner pictures in the ocean, which will ingulf him; if religious aspiration, moral enthusiasm, tender and disinterested sentiments, are but so many follies; if the godly and the fair, are thus wrenched away from our trust;—what ought we else to do, than bend to our necessity in silence, or try as best we may in the passing hour to forget it. A dirge should be for such a life, and not an anthem! The heavens that canopy our globe should not vex us with their gentle stars. The sun should not be so flaming a torch over our funereal dwelling. The trees should not rock their heads so gladly in the wind; the birds should not carol so sweetly among their branches. The flowers are too brilliant for a grave; they should have sadder hues, if they only decorate a pathway to oblivion. If man is an orphan in his infinitude, if there is no shielding about him, if he has no assurance of spiritual realities, — then certainly his isolation is inconceivably awful, his fate is in the midst of lies, existence is but a short passage from silence to silence, — then, certainly, the wretched pilgrimage should be made with a drooping head, and a melancholy face. Such doctrine is that which Byron preaches, and he preaches it with impressive and with gloomy power.

"'Twas strange; — in youth all action and all life,
Burning for pleasure, not averse from strife; —
Woman, the field, the ocean, all that gave
Promise of gladness, peril of a grave,
In turn he tried; he ransacked all below,
And found his recompense in joy and woe, —
No tame, trite medium, — for his feelings sought
In that intenseness, an escape from thought.

The tempest of his heart in scorn had gazed
On that the feeble elements had raised;
The rapture of his heart had looked on high,
And asked, if greater dwelt beyond the sky.
Chained to excess, the love of each extreme,
How woke he from the wildness of that dream!
Alas, he told not; but he did awake,
To curse the withered heart, that would not break."

These lines may stand as a picture of Byron himself; but, if the portrait should be disputed, we take the following, as a statement of his philosophy. If philosophy can be more cheerless, more sorrowful, more despairing, then we may take the atheist's epitaph of "eternal sleep" as the best consolation in human history. Here is our poet's idea of life:

"We wither from our youth, we gasp away
Sick, — sick; unfound the boon, unslaked the thirst,
Though to the last, in verge of our decay,
Some phantom lures, such as we sought at first;
But all too late; so, are we doubly curst.
Love, fame, ambition, avarice, 't is the same, —
Each idle, — and all ill, — and none the worst; —
For all are meteors with a different name,
And death the sable smoke, where vanishes the flame."

Despondency was the natural issue of a genius like Byron's, with Byron's experience. The wretched inadequacy of that experience could not long be concealed. The cup of sensualism, drunk, at first, with zest, and afterwards from habit, when its madness sobered, only left disgust. Celebrity passed from enthusiasm to fashion; and while praises, like a hollow wind, fell empty on his ear, thought strove vainly in his soul with destiny, as a boiling sea in a rayless cavern, that breaks in fury against the rocky barriers which it cannot burst. Passion, divested of sentiment, lost all that concealed its grossness. Affections were a waste. Byron felt with agony the insufficiency of the tangible and the visible; and his agony was the more poignant, that he had nothing in their place. He could weigh, in the balance of a keen philosophy, the pleasures for which men toil, and the prizes for which they fight; he could see that they were lighter than vanity. He was not the dupe of their follies, and yet he did not teach them wisdom. He was not an associate in their idolatries, and yet he did not seek a purer worship. He was an unsparing iconoclast; but when the temple was bare which he had dismantled, and the images which he had broken lay in fragments on the floor, he was himself alone in the wreck, with only the solitary consciousness of power, and the echoes of his own dirge reverberating through the vacant spaces. Genius, to enjoy and to communicate happy and exalting life, must have union with the moral and the spiritual; with the truth which they inspire; with the beauty which they sanctify. These belong to the soul's moral and progressive being; and these, good and fair forever, no genius can exhaust, and no genius can transcend. Genius, therefore, to act in freedom, and in a right direction, must be of faith and love and hope; of the faith which can reverence and can trust; of the love which can receive and give; of the hope which faith and love sustain, which gleams cheeringly over the path of humanity, and which, by large sympathy, has large wisdom. These are the principles which connect us with the universe of highest thought, and of most enduring beauty. It is by faith, that poetry, as well as devotion, soars above this dull earth; that imagination breaks through its clouds, breathes a purer air, and lives in a softer light. It is love that gives the poet the whole heart of man; and it is by love that he speaks to the whole heart of man forever. Hope, which is but our ideal future, lives even in our most prosaic experience, and is a needful solace to our daily toils. We can then but ill spare it from our poetic dreams. We can but ill endure, among so many sad realities, to rob anticipation of its pleasant visions.

In speaking thus, I would not imply that life can be always sunshine. By no means. Its afflictions are many; they are universal; they are inevitable. Because they are so, life can afford to lose none of its alleviations. Much that belongs merely to the present, it must of necessity lose. Wretched it is indeed, if it must likewise resign the future. Much will be carried from us, as our years decline, which years that come never can restore. Hours there are, brief, happy hours, in experience, which may not be forgotten, but are no more to be renewed. They can be but once, and the effort to repeat, is to destroy them. They go to the past as a dream; they are no more, except that now and then their shadows mock us through the mist of days. Pure enjoyments, and bright expectancies, the most meagre souls have known some time in their existence; and the most meagre souls, in feeling that they shall never know them again, are capable of deep regret. They are as a melody when the lute is broken; they are as a tale which the minstrel tells, — and dies. The inanimate universe itself, seems to undergo the changes of our own spirits, and to sympathize with the transitions of our experience. The stars, it is true, rise as brightly in the heavens, the flowers spring as lovely from the earth, the woodlands bloom as freshly as before; but oh, the glory and the joy within, the fancy and the hope, which made the stars more beautiful, and the flowers more graceful, and the woods more elysian, and the birds more musical, will not last with passing suns, nor come back again with returning seasons. I do not decry this characteristic of our nature. I do not decry the genius which has affinity with it, and appeals to it. A high and solemn melancholy is the sighing of our immortality; it is the struggle of a divine aspiration with our earthly imperfections. The capacity of sorrow belongs to our grandeur; and the loftiest of our race are those who have had the profoundest grief; because they have had the profoundest sympathies. There is a sadness which is an attribute of our spiritual humanity; and it is only when this spiritual humanity is dormant, that misery approaches the limitation of simple physical suffering or physical want. To be happy as moral and intellectual beings, we must feel the joy which has its centre in the soul; from that centre springs also the anguish which testifies our exaltation. This very sorrow of ours is one of the strongest reasons why nothing should dissociate the soul from principles which are not dependent on externals, but which, when suns grow dim, will come out into brighter revelation.

Take away faith in the spiritual, and an unhappy mind can find much in visible existence to nourish a philosophy of despair. Byron found abundant food in history, in his own age, and in his own experience, to sustain such a philosophy. It is not my purpose to maintain, that even within narrow limits his philosophy was legitimately constructed ; but life and events, considered with the interpretation of his morbid fancy, were consistent enough with his system. To which side soever he turned, the instability of grandeur, the transiency of power, the vanity of desire were before him ; they were alike evident on the hoary tombs of empires, and on their new-made graves. When he had mused in the Parthenon or Coliseum, in monastic abbey or kingly hall, he came forth from the world of the dead to find a like mortality in the world of the living. It was not that Greece, in her roofless temples and her shattered statues, was covered with the dust of her former beauty ; it was not that Rome, in her wilderness of ruins, presented but the huge, grim skeleton of her giant-corpse ; — the modern Europe of Byron's own observation was a stage of shifting scenes. Thrones had been pulled down in blood ; in blood were thrones built up ; and the crash of the new almost mingled with that of the old. The hopes of liberty grew faint in the crimes of anarchy or the chains of despotism. Ambitiom of colossal stride, that walked in ruin, that marked its way in prints of death, was itself struck down on Waterloo ; and ere the grass was green upon the moistened earth, Byron was there to chant its elegy. The man of Destiny, the man whose name was "Terror," was despoiled in the fortune of an hour; and Byron, who had watched his star with admiration, as it climbed in fiery triumph to its zenith through vapors and through clouds of tears, saw its beams dwindle to a narrow rock, — those beams which had so long showered plagues and death upon the nations. Here was mere man in his pomp and nothingness; here he was for Byron's spirit and Byron's philosophy; for his complaint and sarcasm, for his despondency and for his mockery.

But a strong soul like Byron's could never waste itself in despondency, could never rest in despondency. The aspirations which do not bear a strong soul to content, madden it to resistance. The first expression of despair is complaint, the next is defiance. When enjoyments fail of zest; when desire has turned to bitterness; when disappointment is tired of bewailings; when memory, robbed of feeling, has lost the tenderness of regret, a proud and determined spirit will not brook submission, and will choose nothing but combat. Thus it is in the genius of Byron; the melancholy of "Childe Harold" darkens into the impiety of "Cain"; the reckless criticism of "The English Bards and Scotch Reviewers," hardens into the cynical ribaldry of "Don Juan." Some unthinking persons connect a sort of dignity with mere self-will. This is a low mistake. No principle is more noble, as there is none more holy, than that of a true obedience. Every being is excellent, as it is faithful to the law of its existence. It is by this fidelity in the material universe, that atom holds to atom in solid worlds and in boundless systems. It is by this fidelity in the moral universe, that soul holds to soul in the unity of families and the order of nations. Subvert this fidelity, and where would be beauty? Where even would be existence? Physical or moral anarchy must soon reach its own extinction, in the restoration of order, or the annihilation of the worlds. There would, without obedience, be no kindred to create a home; no law to create a state; there would be no conscience to inspire right; no faith to apprehend religion; humanity, there could be none, nor even the earth to supply it with a dwelling.

The last stage of Byron's genius developed with most potent strength the element of derision. Derision is the worst abuse of genius; and the worst derision is derision of humanity. Byron went on more and more to indulge this acrid temper. He joined the maligners of our species; he trifled with our most sacred feelings; he lacerated the most cherished sensibilities, and in the cruel play of power, he ridiculed the wretches whom he tortured. This is the skepticism of inhumanity, the skepticism of contempt; of all unbelief, the most repulsive and the most evil. There is a skepticism which springs from sympathy; call the sympathy morbid, if you will, it is amiable. It may be in error, but there is kindness at the foundation of its mistake. Nor is it without considerable extenuation. To a mind of more benevolence than faith, there appears much in the world that is startling and inexplicable. Suffering and guilt, the tragedies of passion, the wrongs inflicted, and the wrongs endured, the mysteries of destitution, the pangs of sin, the terrible necessity which so often connects poverty with every other woe,—these evils, to many almost a destiny, which birth is to begin, and life is to fulfil, will sometimes press fearfully on the thoughts of the most believing. There is a moral and sympathetic imagination, which some men have in great activity. They wander, with a singular faculty of realization, among the inequalities of life and the miseries of earth. They conceive vividly of sorrow; they are wounded in the pain of others, and they cannot rest. They ponder on it; they muse over it; and they dream; and their hearts tremble in doubt, while they bleed in pity. The problem of this life must often bring painful suspense to a sensitive mind impatient for the solution. And is not this doubt better than the apathy which often claims the name of faith, and to which the name is too readily conceded? An apathy which does all that the ritual requires, and is at peace in forms; which has not feeling enough to hesitate, which walks its beaten path of hard convention, and looks neither to the right nor to the left; which wraps itself around in the impenetrable cloak of pharisaism, leaving no chink to admit a stray sensibility to annoy its complacency, or to disturb its comfort; which can pass by plundered, prostrate, and wounded man, without the change of a muscle or the wrinkle of a robe. But a skepticism of scorn is yet worse than apathy; a skepticism which originates in bitterness, and goes forth in misanthropy. It is but justice to say of Byron's derision, that it was probably more in affectation than asperity, that his sarcastic mirth was rather from a cheerless than a callous heart; that in a great degree, it was the device of a jaded spirit to conceal the havoc of violent emotion.

Let it not be inferred from the tenor of these remarks, that I undervalue the genius of Byron; such an inference would do me injustice. My object, as I have said, has not been to present a critical estimate, and had I ability to make it, it is now needless. My admiration for the poetic genius of Byron would satisfy his most enthusiastic devotee. The grandeur of it, in its kind, is stupendous. It displays upon occasions a strength which is almost superhuman; yet melody and grace are as much its character as strength. The perception of beauty was in Byron almost an original sense; beauty in all its forms, in external nature, and in the living world. Even when his poetry dejects, it enchants us; it often offends, but it always moves. If Byron's poetry had no other excellence, its vitality will always secure it favor. What life in its descriptions! They people the past. The structures of ancient days arise at the poet's summons, and living figures throng the solitude, and living voices break the silence. The pale marble quickens to emotion; and in the poet's vision, the sculptor's stone is turned to flesh. We see through his words the scorn of Apollo's lip, we glow in the fire of his eye; Venus puts on the light of thought, with the grace of beauty; the gladiator pants to death.

Byron's poetry is eminently reflective. Doubting and desponding as it is, it yet takes interest from the solemn relations of humanity. Though not hopefully, it deals with serious concerns, — the grave, passion, futurity, — and if we are not cheered, we are at least made thoughtful. The fourth canto of "Childe Harold," is a triumph of serious poetry. Solemn music, it comes to the spirit in harmonies of sadness; it comes to the heart in every tone which sounds the deepest to our thoughts, of creation or of destiny.

Byron, in the best moods of his genius, in those moods over which the mocking fiend of cynicism has no control, writes with a most affecting and solemn pathos. That impassioned energy, which fixed attention on its opposite, of absolute rest; that fierce discontent of blood and brain, which can find nothing like such rest in life, made intense to the utmost, by a lonely and dark imagination, brought the sad associations suggested by the tomb into frequent contact with Byron's spirit. Death is, accordingly, a favorite topic with Byron; and his pictures of it, though wanting in the elements which cast over death the deepest tragedy or the purest beauty, that is, a profoundly dramatic force, or the trust of a Christian faith, are yet exceedingly impressive. The closing hours of Manfred; the Prisoner of Chillon's end, as described by his brother; the sombre death of Lara; the lonely death of Medora; the disruption of young life in Zulieka and Haidee, are drawn with surpassing power.

Woman is also a topic around which Byron has lavished an immense wealth of fancy. But the woman of Byron's poetry is a woman of the East and of the South; not woman of the home, but woman of the sun. Woman, in these burning climes, and with the associations which belong to them, suited his impetuous temper and his untrammelled imagination. Woman, thus regarded, he paints with intense warmth of coloring; yet passion is so encircled in gorgeous hues, so decked with graces of the ideal, that, if not free from evil, it is, at least, free from coarseness. While woman is in the fairness of youth and the splendor of loveliness, no poet can surpass Byron in the description of her; and this he has manifested in a series of unrivalled delineations, unrivalled for delicacy and beauty; of Medora, for instance, with her passive enthusiasm; of the Maid of Saragossa, with her daring meekness; of Haidee, with her wild delight; of Aurora Raby, with her saintly sweetness. Byron, however, does not often reach the moral sublime in womanhood; he does not reveal the heart of woman in many of its heroic but unromantic relations. He does not show it to us in the wife growing more into the beauty of faith, as it sobers from the raptures of youth. He does not show it to us in the mother, true to her mission with the care and fidelity of Heaven. He does not show it to us in age venerable in holiness, when the eye that was as morning light is dull with years; when the hair is white, that once was golden as the sun; when hope, long purified in trial and in duty, has transferred its all from this world to the skies. He does not show it to us in martyr-poverty, struggling in want and silence; wasting the bloom of life in toil and sorrow; alleviating the grief of others, and not complaining of its own; bearing in its might of resignation the crushings of affliction that break the strong man to pieces.

Cursory as are these remarks, I cannot omit from them some reference to the conditions of society which surrounded Byron. The short life of Byron was cast in one of the most eventful eras which history records. The beginning of his life was on the margin of the French Revolution, and the close of it was a little later than the fall of Bonaparte. Byron commenced authorship with the century, and ere a quarter of that century was gone, Byron had expired. These were years of doubt and passion, of passion terrible and appalling. The hearts of nations were disturbed. Countries that long had slept awakened in dismay; they started from nightmare to madness. Irreverence took place of faith; and the argument from tradition lost its force for either religion or government. Conflict profound and universal agitated Europe; conflict of ranks, of sentiments, of institutions, of theories, the final result being commonly in physical carnage.

Literature, with certain limitations, is the exponent of the age, and therefore corresponds to it. Social revolutions are, therefore, the periods of impulsive literature. Dante arose amidst the struggles of Italian parties. Milton was the austere genius of English republicanism. Luther came with the Reformation. Shakspeare, Bacon, and a host of others, came soon after. Creation follows dissolution; for with man, creation is but reconstruction. Convention succeeds creation; for imitation comes after invention, and imitation is the soul of custom. The revolution, therefore, which annihilates custom, necessitates invention. Hence it is, that almost every transition in government or society is succeeded by originality in literature. Much there is in literature, as in other things, which is not a spirit, but an occupation; not a mission, but a trade. Many take for granted what others have said before them, and they are vexed if these things are contradicted. Many live by what others before them have done, and they are angry if these things are overturned. So it is in all that constitutes our social life; in government, in creed, in philosophy, in letters. The world, however, moves on in the way of Providence, independently of men's theories and opinions. There is a vitality in truth which cannot be crushed by men's fightings, and which does not die with dissolving systems. Monarchies expire, but government exists; dynasties perish, but rulers are never dead; churches are impoverished, hierarchies are humbled, but religion is not extinguished.

Change there is constantly in the form of life, but

never its destruction. What ought to exist must exist. Kings, priests, and prophets, and workers, the world has, and must have forever. True kings there are, kings of men, whose royalty is not in costume, whose majesty is not in pageants; and these kings have a greatness which is not affected by the fall of empires or the wreck of thrones. True priests there are, whose consecration is not in the visible ceremony, but in the inward preparation, whose mission is as lasting and as wide as man ; and though altars be desecrated, and though shrines be torn, these priests have an anointing which no disruptions can efface, an authority which no violence can despoil. True prophets there are, who will not prolong an echo when the sense is dead, who wait in silence for the living speech, who speak it when it comes, and speak it with enkindled lips. True workers there are, who, through evil report and good, but commonly with more of the evil than the good, still keep busy for their thankless fellows, and when their task is done, lay their tortured or their worn frames where men will weep over the worth which they heeded not while it dwelt amongst them. Byron was eminently a man of the age in its destructive tendencies. He was not the king of it, for he originated and he governed no great movement; he was not the priest of it, for he had no faith and no reverence; he was not the prophet of it, for he had no hope in its advancement; he was not a worker in it, for he joined with no earnest heart in any of the great exertions of philanthropy, which rendered his time an era in man's history. He was simply the pilgrim of the age, walking through its waste places with a solitary spirit, and carrying into the desolate ruins of the past, the morbid passions of the present.

The turbulent agitation with which the poetry of Byron sympathized has not yet subsided. The tendencies which gave that poetry its impulse, are still active. They belong to the force of the free life, which lies at the basis of modern civilization, which daily gains in extent, and gains in strength. The authority of tradition becomes enfeebled before the power of action, and the voice of inquiry has broken the slumbers of submission. Thoughts are going forth in many directions, and each thought has its mission and finds it. Genius has not deserted the arts which give existence enjoyment, and give it grace; but it has drawn the ideal more into union with emotion, and awakened the sentiment of sublimity in the grandeur of the useful. It has bored through solid rocks, and made pathways far from the light of stars or sun. It has chained precipice to precipice, and hung bridges in mid air over the boiling torrent. It has levelled mountains, and exalted valleys. It has assumed dominion over the storm, and become independent of the winds. It has made the ocean a ferry, and spanned continents from border to border with a grasp of iron. It has made the extremities of earth adjacent neighborhoods. It has originated new relations of man to time, to space, and to labor. It has opened a future for speculation, in which the actual results are likely to transcend forever the boldest dreams. The time is not now, and is not to be, when the secluded cloister wins the student to its shade; when the cathedral rises into solemn majesty through the slow growth of a century; when the artist's musings are of loveliness that lives in heaven. The serene faces of saintly tranquillity that look down upon us from ancient canvas with sabbath stillness, have no alliance with the practical and the passionate tendencies of modern genius. But let not conservative taste complain, as if we had nothing in their place. Instead of the cathedral, we have the printing press; instead of the cloister, we have the school. We take not our ideas from moveless structures of symbolic stone, or from storied designings on colored canvas; thought is rendered imperishable as letters, and letters now are as imperishable as man.

Elliott, Byron, and Wordsworth are three poets very different from each other; yet they manifest distinct tendencies which belong to their era.

Elliott, the Corn-law Rhymer, is the bard of manufacturing masses. In him is the cry of their want, and the cry of their strength. Poetry in Elliott is an appeal from starvation. Elliott's spirit is uneasy, dark, discontented, impassioned ; but it is uneasy for the poor, dark with their sorrows, discontented with their lot, and impassioned for their wrongs. Elliott is the poet of toilsmen, of men who ask not for luxury, but life.

Byron, on the contrary, is the poet of those who have exhausted luxury, and wearied of life ; of those, to whom leisure has become a slavery, and indolence a curse ; to whom abundance has become satiety, and pleasure sickness ; of those, to whom existence on this side of the grave is dreary, and all on the other side a blank.

The world to Elliott is a workhouse ; to Byron, it is a banquet-hall, with the feast concluded ; to Wordsworth, it is a place of trial and discipline. Away from the heat of the forge and the noise of the factory ; away from the din of the passions and the laugh of the revel, he meditates on God, where stars are in the lake, and where flowers are in the grass ; he muses on destiny and immortality, where human dust lies silently amidst the mountains. Elliott, however, is nearer to the poor than Wordsworth. Wordsworth condescends to the poor ; Elliott takes his place among them. Wordsworth is their friend; Elliott is their fellow. Wordsworth pities their sufferings; Elliott feels them. The voice of the one is that of sympathy; the voice of the other is that of experience.

And these three poets do not inaptly symbolize conditions of the individual life. Work we must, pleasure we desire; and after work and pleasure, we long for rest and faith. All of us have material wants, and most of us the necessity of toil; but then, we ask for pleasure. Pleasure, however, is short and changeful. It soon fatigues, and then we mourn and despond. At last we supplicate for peace as the highest boon of existence. But labor has its alleviations, and has its recompense. Upon the path of the most toiling there is many a sweet and quiet resting-place, verdant spots decked with flowers, refreshed with streams, where, if we choose, if our inordinate discontents will let us, we may bask in gladness, and forget our cares. Our being has much of sorrow, but so it has passages of happiness unspeakable; the innocence of childhood, the hopes of youth, the nobility of friendship, the generosity of love, the bliss of virtue. Byron's poetry, it is said, has a tendency to sadden us. If it saddened us in the right way, that were no objection. Sadness is not always evil, and sometimes it is wisdom. But there are things to cheer us, things better than Byron's poetry, better than any man's poetry. Nature is better than poetry ; beauty and goodness, truth, kindness, love to God and man, piety and hope are often, in the tired peasant's heart, a richer music than greatest poets ever sung, a music that awakens the seraph's lyre, though it may be faintly heard upon the chill airs of this dull world. Nature is better than poetry ; the images of our goodly universe, that sparkle around us in glorious light ; the sounds that fill God's solemn temple with everlasting harmonies ; the countless orders that with ourselves are quickened by the Creator's spirit ; all this it is given to the simplest to enjoy, it is not given to the most inspired to express. Heaven is yet better than Nature ; Heaven, that ideal of perfect aspiration to which the soul looks up in all its best desires, where it longs to find the consummation of its most ardent yearnings. Better still, unutterably better, the Being, infinite and supreme, the source of all thought, the sum of all excellence, the origin of all truth, the author of all beauty, the life of nature, the light of heaven ; whom the pure in heart can see, and whom in seeing they are blessed forever.

EBENEZER ELLIOTT.

Ebenezer Elliott, the Corn-law Rhymer, the great poet of English artisans, I take for the subject of the present discourse.

My office here is not that of a political economist, but that of a literary critic. My office is to consider rather the poetic genius of my author, than his commercial philosophy. The poetry of Elliott will remain, when the laws against which he so vehemently inveighed will have passed away into the tranquil records of remoter history, and his manly verses will hold a life which in every age the brave and the struggling will recognize and feel. The legislation of Athenians in relation to Macedon has long been silent, but not so the voice of Demosthenes. That rings upon the air of immortality, and in its solemn tones it sounds along from century to century. And the poet is not of weaker or shorter life than the orator. He too will be heard, when the things which aroused his soul shall be known no more. Death quickly unnerves the arm of Köerner, but all ages will sing his "Song of the Sword." The character of Napoleon is fast going to the calm meditation of philosophy and history, but it is with the passion of enthusiasm that French patriots will always chant the burning lyrics of Berenger. The Scots have long since ceased to fight with the Saxons, but through all the future it is in sadness they will pour forth "The Lament on Flodden Field," and in ecstasy "The Ode on Bannockburn." Party politics lose their importance, temporary laws become obsolete; yet if they enkindle the heart of a true poet into a burst of noble song, it continues imperishable in its melody and its strength.

Elliott is an English operative, poetically developed. Let me briefly specify what an English operative is, of ordinary development. The English operative embodies a very decisive form of the English character. He is not speculative, but practical. He is not versatile, but skilful. His sphere is not a large one, but within it he is a master. He is attached to order; he is trained to order, both as a workman and a citizen. Even in revolt, he acts according to a law. He is patient, but not servile. He bears inevitable misfortunes manfully; in the best condition he is sure to grumble, but in the worst he disdains to whine. He is not without aspiration. He is not insensible to dignity; and by many an effort and many a virtue, he makes good a title to nature's nobility. He has much pride of nation. If he glories in nothing else, he glories in his country. Discontented he may be with his rulers, but he is always proud of England. By a generalization, satisfactory at least to himself, he identifies the greatness of England with the power of his own order. The operative classes, in his view, have rendered her the paragon of nations. By them, the earth and the sea are hers, the riches of the mine, and the treasures of the deep. Through the means, he considers, of the operative classes, England governs widely, and governs afar; gains her victories, and maintains her dominion. The English mechanic, even when wanting school instruction, is not wholly ignorant. Knowledge floats around him, of which he cannot but partake; and despite even of himself, the tendency of events subjects him to a progressive education. Associated as he is with large masses, he has community in their intelligence, as well as in their passions. Interests of immediate pressure, which he cannot discard, crowd about him; want, of which he would seek the cause, or for which he would find a remedy, sharpen his sagacity;

theories solicit his belief, and tempt examination; events, discussion, speculation, all that agitate a community profoundly complicated, include his mind in their aggregate activities. When the English mechanic has had his mind opened by reading, he desires to be informed, rather than to be amused; and he is interested in works which treat of society in its principles, rather than in its manners. With reading or without it, he loves nature; he longs for green fields and the wooded lane; he delights in flowers and the song of birds; and he is seldom without a geranium in his garret window, or a trained canary by his working bench.

Such I take to be an honest, but very imperfect estimate of the English mechanic's character. Let me add something on his general condition. In skill the English mechanic has no superior, and none excel him in willingness to work. But still his situation is commonly wretched, and, at best, it is hard. His situation is a hard one, even when his work is constant and certain; for even then, aided by the toil of his children, he can merely earn for the day what the day consumes. The hour, therefore, which finds him idle, or finds him ill, comes to him with want; and the hour which refuses him employment, gives him to pauperism. In his average condition, the British operative is lodged poorly, fed sparingly, and clad imperfectly. He is also the greatest sufferer by the fluctuation of trade, when it is adverse, and the least a gainer when it is prosperous. The turns which bring wealth to the capitalist, afford the operative but a temporary subsistence; while those which injure only the little finger of the capitalist, strike at the very life of the operative. It will be easily inferred, that his intellectual privileges are as few as his physical. He has had no adequate provision for his instruction; no system of education has been presented to him, which he could claim as a right, and accept without degradation. Charity-teaching has, here and there, solicited him to learn; but, in general, charity-teaching, to any wide extent, is worse than ignorance; for it instructs a generation to spell their beggary, and to write themselves slaves. Had educational means been as abundant as they have been scanty, and as elevating as they have been debasing, the British operative could have very imperfectly appropriated them, for his toil began a few steps from the cradle, and it continues till he staggers to the grave. The Sabbath itself is scarcely his inheritance. The Sabbath which was made for man, which was given by the good Father for rest and prayer, has slender greeting from the poor mechanic. Fatigue turns it to apathy, or want clouds it with sorrow. Nor can his children enjoy it as it should be in their power to enjoy it. In a right social state, the Sabbath would be to the young a season of repose, a season of gladness, a weekly jubilee, finding them in happy homes, or at altars free. But no; the youth of the English working classes, to have any escape from absolute ignorance, make it an interval of schooling, and thus, six days' drudgery at the loom is followed by a seventh day's drudgery at the primer.

It is not to be expected that the English mechanic should be contented with his political condition; for however sagacious his exclusion from the suffrage may appear to his ruler, it is too much to think it could be satisfactory to himself. The ruler may decide that he is too poor, too ignorant, or too vicious to be trusted, but such reasons, instead of convincing, insult him. The working man is told, that unless he holds a house of a certain rent he cannot have a vote. But why, he inquires? Every reply directly to this question, implies an injury or an insult. Is it answered that he is ignorant, that he is poor? How comes it, that he should be so ignorant or so poor, that he cannot be permitted to exercise the rights of a citizen? First, he is debased by injustice, and his debasement is then urged against him. Is it answered that he is vicious, and cannot be trusted? The injury is made perfect by insult. But who are you, asks the thinking mechanic, who tell the working poor that they are vicious? You are those who try to tempt our penury; who come to us with the damning bribe; who take base opportunity of our weakness, and wrench from hunger what you would never get from freedom; who corrupt us to sell our souls; and when you have paid the wages of iniquity, turn round, as Satan does on his victims, and scare us with our crime! Those who debauch the few poor that have votes, refuse them to the millions; for such extended franchise would annihilate your power of corruption. Who are you, who tell the working poor that they are vicious? An idle aristocracy; men who feast in the midst of want, and who would keep closed the gates of plenty; men who revel in luxury, and who lay least restraint on their passions; among many of whom sensuality is so notorious, that it has ceased to be scandalous. You are the men, who presume to insinuate that a hard working mechanic has not moral qualification to be a free man upon his birth-soil.

Do you tell the operative that he has no stake in the country? What, no stake? Has he not himself? Has he not his life? Has his life been rendered so miserable, that it is worth nothing even to himself? Has he not, then, kindred — the father who carried him in boyhood, the mother who nursed him in infancy? Has he not a wife and children, as dear to his forlorn heart as if he were a peer? And will you tell the muscular men of England in the hour of need, that they have no stake in the country ; that their partners and little ones do not out-value the world, titles, thrones, and all its other baubles? Did you tell this to the victors of the Nile, or the heroes of Waterloo? Was this your watchword upon the heights of Corunna or the walls of Badajoz? But the working man knows, that base as these imputations against him seem, they are not sincere; he knows, that it is not his ignorance that is feared, but his intelligence ; not his vice, but his independence; it is because that he does appreciate his stake in the country, that he is precluded from manifesting the sense he entertains of its worth. Yet he does not separate this from the rights of others; it is his interest to hold sacred the rights of all classes ; and no calumny is more unfounded than that which would ascribe indifference to the claims of property to the English operatives. The untouched inclosures of the nation ; the abodes of elegance at every turn ; the castles of grandeur that crown so many forests; the secure luxury of nobles in the sight of dying multitudes; the tranquil order of business, give a universal lie to this aspersion!

Jealous of practical liberty, the English masses are not easily disturbed about speculative liberty. They cannot be aroused by abstract ideas; they are stirred to action only by palpable grievances. Chartism is therefore, the exponent of profound and extended suffering; it is no offspring of theoretical reasoning, but of physical endurance; the evil is radical and national. Chartism is a simultaneous cry, not by preconcerted design, but in the unity of a common sorrow, for a remedy as radical and as national as the evil. The Chartists are not, as many suppose, the lowest of the working classes; they are not the disorderly and the ignorant; they are the most sober and the most intelligent. They are men, who, being aware of the support which they afford to the nation, feel entitled to a political existence; they are willing to be members of society, but not its victims.

Physically, then, intellectually, morally, and politically, the condition of English mechanics has long been one of irritation and discontent. Ebenezer Elliott, became the impersonation of this discontent. His voice was raised for millions who had no voice. Dumb under the goad, they found in their brother a heart of pity and a tongue of power. Elliott's voice was mighty, and mighty in complaint. Elliott cried aloud, and spared not. With impetuous and ringing tones, with the stern boldness of an ancient seer, and the vehement eloquence of a modern reformer, he denounced the hard-handed and the proud. He summoned them to trial; he hung up, as witness against them, the skinny skeleton of hunger; he evoked the fiend of want to scare them at their feasts; and he breathed into his terrible verses, the howl of starving multitudes, imploring vindication and relief. We must not regard Elliott as a mere poet. He is a prophet. He needs not fear criticism; but a critical judgment of him, would not be the true judgment. A moral feeling, rather than one of art, must guide our thoughts. He wrote for the suffering; and to the suffering he has clung. He has devoted rare abilities to that side in the social struggle, which, personally, could promise him neither victory nor spoils. "I am sufficiently rewarded," he says, "if my poetry has led one, poor, despairing victim of misrule, from the ale-house to the fields; if I have been chosen of God, to show his desolate heart, that though his wrongs have been heavy, and his fall deep, and though the spoiler is yet abroad, still in the green lanes of England, the primrose is blowing, and on the mountain top the lonely fir is pointing with her many fingers to our Father who is in heaven; to Him whose wisdom is at once inscrutable and indubitable; to whom ages are as a moment; to Him, who has created another and a better world, for all who act nobly and suffer unjustly here; a world of river-feeding mountains, to which the oak will come in his strength and the ash in her beauty ; of chiming streams and elmy vales, where the wild flowers of our country, and among them the little daisy, will not refuse to bloom."

The distinctive characteristic of Elliott as a poet, is strength ; strength of idea, and strength of word ; strength in concentration of thought and in singleness of purpose. Elliott has strength, and he has also the directness which accompanies strength. The courage which belongs to the strong is, therefore, a natural quality of Elliott. Fearless and uncompromising, impassioned and sincere, he is, of course, individual and independent. He is confident of the power that is in him ; he is confident of its worth, and he is honest in its direction. He is the creature of no patron ; he is the pet of no coterie ; he is simply a man of deep feelings and of earnest words ; a man that writes because necessity is laid upon him, and because his heart is full.

But mere strength will not make a poet ; nor will enthusiasm, added to strength, make a poet. To be a poet, a man must have a sense of the beautiful ; and he must have capacity to express this emotion. Elliott feels the beautiful in creation, and hence his delight in nature. The rural sentiment is ever active in his breast. Nature is dear to him, and nature, especially as manifested in the English landscape. The fancy of

Elliott seldom transcends his sympathies. He wanders not through space in the chariot of Queen Mab; a ramble by a native rivulet contents him. He flies not to the vales of Indus, or to the bowers of Samarcand; he is satisfied with the velvet fields, and the sheltered lanes of England. He paints entirely from observation, and therefore his pictures are all from the scenery of his country. His descriptions are fresh and striking; at times, perhaps, elaborate, but never unnatural. His images are excellent, and they are numerous. Occasionally redundant, but always vigorous, they are as different from the conceits of sentimentalism, as mountain oaks from hot-house plants; they are vital forms, not colored shadows; the drapery of living beauty, not wreaths on the brow of a corpse, or garlands hung upon a tomb.

This sympathy with natural objects is a most salutary element in such a mental constitution as that of Elliott. It is this that leads him from the forges to the hill-side, and from the crowded street to the quiet valley. It finds him companions in trees and flowers; it gives him pleasant music in the songs of the grove and the ripple of the stream. It is, therefore, a relief to us, when he takes us from corn laws and cotton lords to peaceful haunts beyond the smoke of town; haunts that soothe the turmoil of his thoughts, and brighten the spirit of his dreams. Though he may still carry with him the tale of his grievance, we love to hear it under the equal and the open sky, rather than in garret or cellar, foundery or mill. Alive as Elliott is to social disorders and social wrongs, it is also well that he should be alive to things which the passions of the fighting world cannot mar. It is well that an ear so tortured with the groans of man, should often give itself to the hymn of nature. It is well that an eye so familiar with the sinful parts of earth, should find a region of consolation which wickedness cannot defile. The breeze upon the cheek; the free winds making choral harmonies with the forest; the joy of animals; the blessed influences of holy light, tend mightily to cleanse the bosom from foul and perilous stuff; to wash from the sicklied brain the corrosions which it has gathered by unhealthy thoughts. Amidst the mountains, beside the ocean, upward among the stars, our mean irritations expire; they are lost in the presence of majesty and vastness; our concentrating littleness is absorbed in the silent immensity of lustre.

Sympathy with external nature also influences the character of Elliott's religion. The piety of Elliott is not ritual, but primitive. He worships God, not in human forms, but in his own consecrated universe. In the spirit of a worshipper, he seeks the copse or dell;

in such a spirit he strolls by the river, or muses in the shade. The spirit of devotion breaks through the roughest of Elliott's denouncings; it comes ever and ever, like a hymn in the mountains between the gusts of a thunder-storm. Darkly as social existence is reflected in his thoughts, he does not leave out from his faith, that a wise and gracious Providence cares for humanity. With the wealthy he is often angry; even with the poor he is, at times, impatient; but before his Maker he is always humble and believing. Elliott dwells but too constantly in the land of Mesech, and sojourns amid the tents of Kedar; the forms most present to his sight and to his musings, are those of faded women and despairing men; but still he holds fast in his piety, and bows in reverence to his Maker in mournful submission. In Elliott's lines on "Forest Worship," we have a fair illustration of his devotional temper. Though shaded with his habitual gloom, there are beamings through them of hope and resignation.

"Within the sun-lit forest,
Our roof the bright blue sky;
Where fountains flow and wild flowers blow,
We lift our hearts on high.
Beneath the frown of wicked men
Our country's strength is bowing,
But thanks to God, they can't prevent
The lone wild flowers from blowing.

"High, high above the tree-tops
The lark is soaring free;
Where streams the light through broken clouds,
His speckled breast I see:
Beneath the might of wicked men
The poor man's worth is dying;
But thank'd be God, in spite of them,
The lark still warbles flying.

"The preacher prays, Lord bless us!
Lord bless us, echo cries;
Amen, the breezes murmur low,
Amen, the rill replies:
The ceaseless toil of woe-worn hearts
The proud with pangs are paying:
But here, O God of earth and heaven!
The humble heart is praying.

"How softly in the pauses
Of song, re-echoed wide,
The cushat's coo, the linnet's lay,
O'er hill and river glide.
With evil deeds, of evil men,
The affrighted land is ringing;
But still, O Lord! the pious heart
And soul-toned voice are singing."

Imagination, in its creative force, does not, as I apprehend, belong to Elliott; but fancy is his; fancy that teems with poetic illustration, and that burns with eloquent impulses. Yet though the fancy of Elliott is strong and rich, it is not plastic ; and this appears especially in his management of numbers and language. His verse wants music ; it is obstinate ; rugged ; of difficult enunciation. It is pervaded with fire ; it is not a fire, however, which renders expression liquid, but a fire which makes it hard ; it does not give to language harmony, but intensity. Elliott is copious, but not select; and though evidently master of an abundant vocabulary, he uses favorite epithets and phrases with a constancy of repetition, which would be intolerable in a writer of less ability. There is an artistic command by which the poet uses words as the painter uses colors ; by which his verses become to the ear what a picture is to the eye ; by which variety and sweetness of modulation have similar effects to a just disposition of light and shade ; by which diction commingles into one the spirit of thought and the beauty of the universe. Such I apprehend to be the essence of poetic harmony. This is not, as I conceive, the distinctive excellence of Elliott. I say distinctive, because I would not assert that Elliott never has it. Occasionally, his verse has a gentle sweetness or a high choral sounding, which would entitle it to a lofty place in the music of poetry.

In the nature of his topics, Elliott has some resemblance to Crabbe. Both have selected their subjects from humble life; and both have dealt with their subjects in a tone of earnestness, and conformably to reality. Here the resemblance closes. Elliott admits the suggestive action of Crabbe's genius upon his mind, yet Elliott is not his imitator. He has more passion than Crabbe, more fancy, and more sympathy. His verse, assuming every diversity of structure, does not contain the variety of incident which quivers beneath the simple and monotonous lines of Crabbe. He is not, like Crabbe, minute and literal; nor has he Crabbe's fearful power of tragic narrative. He cannot, as that writer, work up a picture of sin and sorrow, until the heart is chill; he cannot freeze the blood, but he can heat it; he can kindle anger, but he cannot inspire terror.

I have said, that Elliott has great love for external nature; he has, also, great love for man. This love has been rendered angry by his circumstances; it has been turned into indignation by the wrong which humanity inflicts upon humanity. He has companioned with the afflicted, and he has taken up the burden of their lamentation, and their curse. He is, therefore, a prophet in the wilderness of calamity, and his voice is as sad as it is vehement. There is a mighty heart in the man, but the big veins of it are filled with grief; they swell with a huge suffering, and groans not loud, but deep, come out of the heavings. The brotherhood of Elliott have literally been "men of sorrows," and Elliott's is a temper to make such sorrow all his own. He had no need to stir his imagination with thoughts of fictitious woe; the presence of actual misery was always before him. It met him at every turn; it stared on him at every corner; it pressed on him at every sense; it peered up to him from the foggy cellar; it gazed down upon him from the dizzy garret; he heard it in the whine of breadless childhood; he saw it in the pale faces which crowded from the nightly factory to meet the sleepy dawn; it sat before him in the worn mother with her sickly infant; it staggered by him in the drooping father leading out his consumptive boy, to lie upon the grass, and pluck a flower ere he died. How could a man like Elliott, a man, almost made of fire, escape being stirred to fury? How was any temperance of humanity preserved in him? Only, because he had pity equal to his anger, and his weeping was even more bitter than his wrath.

What a martyrdom for life is his, who cannot help but feel? Who cannot escape from the wretchedness about him, nor yet from the sensibility within, which gives to that wretchedness its utmost gloom? There is, to be sure, an idealism, which discerns a glorious hope, or the state would not be martyrdom, but perdition. The martyr, in the midst of agonies, sees the heavens opened, and the light streaming down upon him from the throne of God ; and in the very chokings of torture, he puts forth the anthems of faith. The poet has such faith in the worst of hours ; and poets such as Elliott need it. His song is truly the hymn of the martyr. A vast difference, there is, between imaginary woes, and the woes of imagination ; a vast difference between the regrets of a coquette for the loss of a worthless lover, and the grief of that man who can hear the prisoner's sigh in the lowest dungeon of earth, who can realize in its terrible extent the empire of wrong, upon which, indeed, the sun never sets. To speak simply of personal afflictions, how exceeding heavy are they on the man of imagination, in whom there is a true sensibility. To mere instinct they are soon over. They are clouds that spread shadows as they pass, but are melted in the first gush of the sun. With imagination, in which the heart's life keeps fresh, they are spectres that disappear, but come back again at the slightest touch.

The vividness and intensity which belong to genius, are sources of perennial suggestiveness. The common mind, dependent ever on the senses, weeps away its grief in the hour when it comes, but to the strong and keen imagination, sorrow starts up from the grave of years, more killing than ever in its first visitation. Often the man of genius seems to want ordinary sensibility while affliction is present; his voice is firm, and his eye holds no tear; but when the event is nothing to those who moaned the loudest, it will come back to him; it will cross the paths of his solitary walks; it will sit by him in his thoughtful indolence; it will lean with him over the declining embers; it will start on him in the midst of his reasonings; it will interrupt his meditations with sobbings as of a child. What, then, must life have been to such a man as Elliott? With a heart that could not be otherwise than unhappy, while his fellows groaned; with that capacity which gathered into its range of perception, the cotton mill, the forge, the ten thousand varieties of poor men's homes, the bald monotony of poor men's histories, the hopeless fardel of toil and destitution, how could he be othewise than sad; his bosom a fountain of tears, and his utterance a voice of wailing! I will not say, that Elliott's gloom is desirable either for poetry or usefulness. It is well, indeed, that there should be always souls to burn for evils that are rampant in the habitable world; it is well there should be a sympathy, which will not hold its peace, while the weak are crushed; it is well there should be an anger which will not quit the warfare against injustice, while injustice triumphs. Yet, for strong and healthy action, there must be points of rest, and many associations of peace ; there must be serene spaces, from which the soul can shut out the cares that oppress it. Even to ameliorate the disorders for which we grieve, and to acquire energy against them, we must often take ourselves away from their company. Sympathy, itself, droops in an unvarying contemplation of wretchedness ; and therefore, to sustain the mission of philanthropists, we must carry the cheerfulness of hope into the toils of mercy. I will not say, that the feelings of Elliott are not often too prejudiced and one-sided. The poet must be more than an advocate. The anger of the poet like that of the prophet, must be an anger more solemn than that of the passions. The poet, too, who wishes to outlive the strifes of a generation, must have that tolerance which marks the permanent and the comprehensive manifestations of humanity; he must have the eye of wisdom, and the heart of charity. The poor man, however, so absorbs Elliott, so attracts his sympathy, that the rich man has little from him but resistance. He forgets, too often, that humanity, in the peer as in the beggar, is a thing of frailties, subject to folly and to grief; a thing which, under the brightest gaud, bears anguish enough to claim our pity.

Elliott has been a fertile writer. His productions I cannot minutely examine, or even specify. Among his shorter poems, there are some that come out from the heart's fulness, and speak at once to the heart's sympathies. Among these I may mention, "The Dying Boy to the Sloe Blossom," "Mary's Dream," "Preston Mills," "He went, He wrote, He came." Elliott has had woe and trials in his own home; he has wept on the waste spaces which death made in his little circle; and in all these expressions of grief-inspired genius, we feel the man in the poet, and the poet in the man. "The Village Patriarch" is the longest poem of Elliott, and perhaps his best. It is thoughtful and elevated. Enoch Wray, the village patriarch, has numbered a hundred years. A humble man was Enoch Wray. He was poor, but had genius. He had the wisdom of the head, and the cunning of the hand; his speaking and his work showed he had ideas, and that these ideas were his own. In his youth he became blind by too intense a perusal of Schiller's drama of "The Robbers;" the French Revolution having increased the agitation, until it destroyed his sight. When the poet introduces us to the old man eloquent, he is the chronicle of his neighborhood, the impersonation of a century. The glory of the world has departed from his eye, but truth and wisdom are a more excellent glory to his soul. The beauty of things visible has given place to the beauty of things immortal.

He is resigned, but despondent; his home has been afflicted, and his country has become degenerate. England, he thinks, is not the England of his youth. The peasants are sparingly fed, and the nobles are no longer generous. But nature is ever dear to Enoch. He loves the odor of the primrose, and the texture of the violet; he loves to sit in summer by his cottage door, and to feel the breath of evening upon his sightless brow. He loves with friendly help to climb the mountain, and there, upon its lonely summit, amidst the silence of infinitude, to commune with the Eternal. Enoch soon walks no more with man. After some gropings to familiar places, after some farewells to old companions, Enoch gives up the ghost, and is gathered to his fathers. The whole poem is impressed with genius, but the whole must be read that the genius may be felt. Enoch's own character is shrouded in a dim religious grandeur; with impassioned lamentation, there are gentle musings that tell of hard days passed in toil, and quiet Sabbaths passed in prayer; there are elevation and seriousness, the elevation of a solemn faith, and the seriousness of a profound experience.

The Corn-law Rhymes, are the verses by which Elliott is most extensively known; and though by no means the best of his works, they are those which give him his literary designation. They are verses of extraordinary power; but of power to be thoroughly understood only by those who know the poverty of England. These poems are fierce, scornful, indignant, sarcastic, sweeping boldly along in thundering rebuke, or fiery denunciation. Take this battle song as an instance — and I think it is a fair one — of their spirit and their energy:

"Day, like our souls, is fiercely dark;
What then? 'T is day!
We sleep no more; the cock crows — hark!
To arms! away!

"They come! they come! the knell is rung
Of us or them;
Wide o'er their march the pomp is flung
Of gold and gem.

"What collar'd hound of lawless sway,
To famine dear —
What pensioned slave of Attila,
Leads in the rear?

"Come they from Scythian wilds afar,
Our blood to spill?
Wear they the livery of the Czar?
They do his will.

"Nor tassell'd silk, nor epaulette,
Nor plume, nor torse —
No splendor gilds, all sternly met,
Our foot and horse.

"But, dark and still we inly glow,
Condensed in ire!
Strike, tawdry slaves, and ye shall know
Our gloom is fire.

"In vain your pomp, ye evil powers,
Insults the land;
Wrongs, vengeance, and the cause is ours!
And God's right hand!

"Mad men! They trample into snakes
The wormy clod!
Like fire, beneath their feet awakes
The sword of God!

"Behind, before, above, below,
They rouse the brave —
Where'er they go, they make a foe
Or find a grave."

But they are not all thus. Here is a rhyme of more sober character:

"Wrong not the laboring poor by whom ye live,
Wrong not your humble fellow-worms, ye proud!
For God will not the poor man's wrongs forgive,
But hear his plea, and have his plea allowed.

"O be not like the vapors, splendor-rolled,
That, sprung from earth's green breast, usurp the sky.
Then spread around contagion black and cold
Till all who mourn the dead, prepare to die!

"No! imitate the bounteous clouds that rise,
Freighted with bliss from river, vale, and plain;
The thankful clouds that beautify the skies,
Then fill the lap of earth with fruit and grain.

"Yes! emulate the mountain and the flood,
That trade in blessings with the mighty deep;
Till, soothed to peace, and satisfied with good,
Man's heart be happy as a child asleep."

And here is a truly noble chant on "The Press:"

"God said, 'Let there be light;'
Grim darkness felt his might
And fled away;
Then startled seas and mountains cold
Shone forth, all bright in blue and gold,
And cried — ''T is day, 't is day.'

"Hail, holy light! exclaimed
The thund'rous cloud that flamed
O'er daisies white;
And lo! the rose in crimson dressed,
Leaned sweetly on the lily's breast;
And blushing, murmured—'Light!'

"Then was the sky-lark born,
Then rose the embattled corn;
Then floods of praise
Flowed o'er the sunny hills of noon;
And then, in stillest might, the moon
Poured forth her pensive lays.

"Lo! heaven's bright bow is glad,
Lo, trees and flowers, all clad
In glory, bloom!
And shall the mortal sons of God
Be senseless as the trodden clod,
And darker than the tomb!

"No! by the *mind* of man!
By the swart artisan!
By God our Sire!
Our souls have holy light within,
And every form of grief and sin,
Shall see and feel its fire.

"By earth, and hell, and heaven,
The shroud of souls is riven,

Mind, mind alone
Is light, and hope, and life, and power!
Earth's deepest night from this bless'd hour,
The night of mind, is gone!

"The Press all lands shall sing;
The Press, the Press we bring,
All lands to bless;
O pallid Want! O Labor stark!
Behold, we bring the sacred ark!
The Press! the Press! the Press!"

Elliott has the poetic nature in him in its elemental strength; but he differs from most poets as to the manner in which it works through him, and in which it finds expression. Elliott seems to feel a passion in its utmost power, then to be troubled for its limitations, until he becomes angry unto wrath, or saddened to despair, for the wronged or the wretched, in whom nature is either maddened or destroyed. Take a case. Wordsworth's heart leaps up when he beholds a rainbow in the sky. Elliott, with as deep appreciation, would feel his heart bowed down. Wordsworth would find companions in the stones and sheep, to gaze with him, and to enjoy the sight. Elliott would think of men, with hearts like his own, who had not often seen a rainbow, or the sun that makes one. Take another case. In the gallows, with all its terrible and retributive associations, Wordsworth beholds the solemn action of society upon guilt, and he pours around it the mystic halo of his genius in high-sounding sonnets. Were it not almost profane, we might call some of them the Hangman's Hymns. Elliott would see in the gallows, especially the English gallows, the fatal consummation of a social tragedy, in which the poor were victims, — the poor, ignorant by neglect, vicious by ignorance, and exterminated by vice.

Take one case more. " Love " is with all poets a universal passion ; and in prose and verse it is the inspiration of all that is ideal and imaginative in literature. Elliott's very heart is on fire with it, and strike the chord as poet may, no bard sounds a higher note than his. But bards in general warble the song as one in which all beings can join chorus, the captive with the king, the beggar with the bird. Elliott, feeling the truth and power of love in his own soul, but in an equal degree knowing, from practical sympathy, how the oppressed are deprived of it, sings rather differently. He is right, most right ; for a slave there is no genuine love, and bravely thus, and honestly, he chants it :

"Slaves! where ye toil for tyrants, Love is not:
Love's noblest temple is the freeman's cot!
What though each blast its humble thatch uptear,
Bold shall the tyrant be that enters there.
Look up and see, where, throned on Alpine snow,
Valor disdains the bondsman's vales below:
So, Love, companion of the wolf, may roam,
And in the desert find a boundless home;
But will not bow the knee to pomp and pride,
Where slaves of slaves with hate and fear reside.
What are the glories that Oppression throws
Around his vainly-guarded throne of woes;
The marbles of divinity, and all
That decks pale Freedom's pomp of funeral?
Let Grandeur's home, o'er subject fields and floods,
Rise, like a mountain clad in wintry woods,
And columns tall, of marble wrought, uphold
The spiry roof, and ceilings coved in gold;
But better than the palace and the slave
Is Nature's cavern that o'erlooks the wave,
Rock-paved beneath, and granite-arched above,
If Independence sojourn there with Love!"

Elliott, in description, overlays his subject. He is prolific and luxuriant to a fault. The characteristic beauties of an object, or a scene, are lost in his profusion and his amplitude. But perhaps this is more than compensated for by his wild wealth of power. Out of this he pours a prodigal irregularity, even as Nature herself pours it. Elliott makes poor work when he attempts humor. It is the elephant essaying the gambols and grimaces of the monkey. His mind is too large, too massive, and too unwieldy for the lighter graces of humor. It is too sad, too earnest, too dark, too passionate, for the gigantic banter, the Polyphemus-like laughter of Pantagruelism. It is too tender, too full of sympathy and humanity, for the sardonic and sarcastic ridicule of Mephistophelianism. Pensive in the field, excited in the crowd, mixing sensations and impressions from both with the workings of his fine but sombre imagination, and with the pantings of his strong but gentle heart, he becomes truly great; great, because then he combines his poetic with his actual life; and therein consists his power. He is a Titanic workman, singing his terrible song of Labor. He is the Æschylus of toil. He is the solemn tragic genius of England's artisans. Hood was the female-mind of those who earn Death by the sweat of the brow. Of such, Elliott is the masculine mind. The genius of Elliott is to that of Hood, as the song of the sledge would be to "The Song of the Shirt;" and yet, withal, he has ever and again tones of such sweetness as need a pen dipped in tears to write them. Here is a gush of this kind:

" The meanest thing to which we bid adieu,
Loses its meanness in the parting hour.
When long-neglected worth seems born anew,
The heart that scorns earth's pageantry and power
May melt in tears, or break, to quit a flower."

Then hear this scathing, this fierce, this indignant cry :

" Shall *I*, lost Britain ! give the pest a name
That, like a cancer, eats into thy core ?
'T is Avarice, hungry as devouring flame ;
But swallowing all, it hungers as before,
While flame, its food exhausted, burns no more.
O ye hard hearts that grind the poor, and crush
Their honest pride, and drink their blood in wine,
And eat their children's bread without a blush,
Willing to wallow in your pomp, like swine,
Why do ye wear the human form divine ?
Can ye make men of brutes, contemn'd, enslav'd ?
Can ye grow sweetness on the bitter rue ?
Can ye restore the health of minds deprav'd ?
And self-esteem in blighted hearts renew ?
Why should souls die to feed such worms as you ?
Numidian ! who didst say to hated Rome, —
' There is no buyer yet to purchase thee ! '
Come, from the damn'd of old, Jugurtha, come !
See one Rome fall'n ! — another, mightier, see !
And tell us what the second Rome shall be !

But long, O Heav'n! avert from this sad land
The conflict of the many with the few,
When, crumpled, like a leaf, in havock's hand,
The great, the old, shall vanish from the view,
And slaves be men, all traitors, and all true!
Nor from the fierce and iron-breathing North,
That grimly blossoms with the sword and spear,
Call a new Alaric and his robbers forth,
To crush what worth is left untrampled here,
And shake from Freedom's urn dust still too dear,
While trade-left Thames pours mute his shipless wave!"

An excellent aphorism is the following couplet, one that should live in the hearts of statesmen:

"For they who fling the poor man's worth away,
Root out security, and plant dismay."

Elliott, poet as he is, nay, just because he is a poet, cannot see all deformity in the steam-fed city. Poetry is not all beauty. Poetry is power, freedom, and passion as well. Indeed, beauty is subordinate in comparison to these. Whatever exhibits human power in connection with human passion, has poetry in it, and greatest poetry. It is in cities, therefore, that the mightiest of poets have been trained. Steam is a marvellous agency, an almost miraculous adaptation of man's invention to man's wants. It were strange if the poets in the nineteenth century could pass it over, or only find it prosaic and repulsive. Elliott could not do so; and his lines accordingly, on "Steam at Sheffield," are among the grandest and the most inspired of his compositions. Steam does not, as some assert, put man behind the mechanism. Not so. *Man is in the mechanism.* What is man at any time without a machine? But steam becomes more and more united with man's life, and interests, and fate; and I repeat, it were strange, passing strange, if out of these no poetry could be extracted:

"Oh, there is glorious harmony in this
Tempestuous music of the giant, Steam,
Commingling growl, and roar, and stamp, and hiss,
With flame and darkness! Like a Cyclop's dream,
It stuns our wondering souls, that start and scream
With joy and terror; while, like gold on snow,
Is morning's beam on Andrew's hoary hair!
Like gold on pearl is morning on his brow!
His hat is in his hand, his head is bare;
And, rolling wide his sightless eyes, he stands
Before this metal god, that yet shall chase
The tyrant idols of remotest lands,
Preach science to the desert, and efface
The barren curse from every pathless place."

"The Ranter" is a noble strain, and in the highest mood of Elliott's genius. Here is a blast trumpet-toned on the Puritan pilgrims:

"O for a Saint, like those who sought and found,
For conscience' sake, sad homes beyond the main!
The Fathers of New England, who unbound,
In wild Columbia, Europe's double chain:
The men whose dust cries, 'Sparta, live again!'
The slander'd Calvinists of Charles's time
Fought (and they won it) Freedom's holy fight.
Like prophet-bards, although they hated rhyme,
All incorruptible as heaven's own light,
Spoke each devoted preacher for the right.
No servile doctrines, such as power approves,
They to the poor and broken-hearted taught;
With truths that tyrants dread, and conscience loves,
They wing'd and barb'd the arrows of their thought;
Sin in high places was the mark they sought;
They said not, 'Man be circumspect and thrive!
Be mean, base, slavish, bloody—and prevail!'
Nor doth the Deity they worshipp'd drive
His four-in-hand, applaud a smutty tale,
Send Members to the House, and us to gaol.
With zeal they preach'd, with reverence they were heard;
For in their daring creed, sublime, sincere,
Danger was found, that parson-hated word!
They flatter'd none—they knew nor hate nor fear,
But taught the will of God—and *did it* here.

Even as the fire-wing'd thunder rends the cloud,
Their spoken lightnings, dazzling all the land,
Abash'd the foreheads of the great and proud,
Still'd faction's roar, as by a god's command,
And meeken'd Cromwell of the iron hand."

I cannot fancy any words that toil-starved poverty can conceive of sadder pathos than this low plaint:

SONG.

TUNE — "*The Land o' the Leal.*"

"Where the poor cease to pay,
Go, lov'd one, and rest!
Thou art wearing away
To the land of the blest.
Our father is gone
Where the wrong'd are forgiven,
And that dearest one,
Thy husband, in heaven.

"No toil in despair,
No tyrant, no slave,
No bread-tax is there,
With a maw like the grave.
But the poacher, thy pride,
Whelm'd in ocean afar;
And his brother who died
Land-butcher'd in war;

"And their mother, who sank
  Broken-hearted to rest;
And the baby, that drank
  Till it froze on her breast;
With tears, and with smiles,
  Are waiting for thee,
In the beautiful isles
  Where the wrong'd are the free.

"Go, loved one, and rest
  Where the poor ceased to pay!
To the land of the blest
  Thou art wearing away;
But the son of thy pain
  Will yet stay with me,
And poor little Jane
  Look sadly like thee."

An extract from a poem entitled "Win-Hill,"* or "The Curse of God," will show to what sublimity Elliott can attain:

"Thy voice is like thy Father's, dreadful storm!
  Earth hears his whisper, when thy clouds are torn!
And Nature's tremor bids our sister-worm
  Sink in the ground. But they who laugh to scorn

---

* The central mountain—not the highest—of the Peak of Derbyshire.

The trampled heart which want and toil have worn,
Fear thee, and laugh at HIM, whose warning word
Speaks from thy clouds, on burning billows borne;
For, in their hearts, his voice they never heard,
Ne'er felt his chastening hand, nor pined with hope deferr'd.

"O Thou whose whispering is the thunder! Power
Eternal, world-attended, yet alone!
O give, at least, to labor's hopeless hour
That peace, which Thou deny'st not to a stone!
The famine-smitten millions cease to groan;
When wilt Thou hear their mute and long despair?
Lord, help the poor! for they are all thy own.
Wilt Thou not help? did I not hear Thee swear
That Thou would'st tame the proud, and grant their victim's prayer?

"Methought I saw THEE in the dreams of sleep.
This mountain, Father, groan'd beneath thy heel!
Thy other foot was placed on Kinder's steep;
Before thy face I saw the planets reel,
While earth and skies shone bright as molten steel;
For under all the stars Thou took'st thy stand,
And bad'st the ends of heaven behold and feel,
That thou to all thy worlds had'st stretch'd thine hand,
And curs'd for evermore the Legion-Fiend of Land!"

And now a gentle tone:

"Sleep, sleep, my love! thy gentle bard
Shall wake, his fevered maid to guard:

The moon in heaven rides high;
The dim stars through thy curtains peep;
Whilst thou, poor sufferer, triest to sleep,
They hear thy feeble cry.

"She sleeps! but pain, though baffled, streaks,
With intermitting blush, her cheeks,
And haunts her troubled dream:
Yet shalt thou wake to health, my love,
And seek again the blue-bell'd grove,
And music-haunted stream."

Take the following as a specimen of Elliott's pathos:

THE BROKEN HEART.

"Stop, passenger! for I am weak,
And heavy are my falling feet—
Stop! till I gather strength to speak:
Twice have I seen thee cross the street,
Where woe and wild-flowers seldom meet.

"O give a pallid flower to her
Who ne'er again will see one grow!
Give me a primrose, passenger!
That I may bless it ere I go
To my false love, in death laid low.

"Sweet—sweet! it breathes of Rother's bowers,
Where, like the stream, my childhood play'd;
And, happy as the birds and flowers,

My love and I together strayed,
Far from the dim town's deadly shade.

"Why did he leave my mother's cot?
My days of trouble then began:
I followed, but he knew me not!
The stripling had become a man!
And now in heaven he waits for Ann.

"Back from consumption's streeted gloom,
To death's green fields, I fain would fly;
In yon churchyard there is no room
For broken-hearted flowers to sigh,
And look on heaven before they die."

Yet here is an illustration, if possible, more touching:

THE DYING BOY TO THE SLOE BLOSSOM.

"Before thy leaves thou com'st once more,
White blossom of the sloe!
Thy leaves will come as heretofore;
But this poor heart, its troubles o'er,
Will then lie low.

"A month at least before thy time
Thou com'st, pale flower, to me;
For well thou know'st the frosty rime
Will blast me ere my vernal prime,
No more to be.

"Why here in winter? No storm lowers
O'er Nature's silent shroud!
But blithe larks meet the sunny showers,
High o'er the doomed untimely flowers
In beauty bowed.

"Sweet violets, in the budding grove,
Peep where the glad waves run;
The wren below, the thrush above,
Of bright to-morrow's joy and love
Sing to the sun.

"And where the rose-leaf, ever bold,
Hears bees chant hymns to God,
The breeze-bowed palm, mossed o'er with gold,
Smiles on the well in summer cold,
And daisied sod.

"But thou, pale blossom, thou art come,
And flowers in winter blow,
To tell me that the worm makes room
For me, her brother, in the tomb,
And thinks me slow.

"For as the rainbow of the dawn
Foretells an eve of tears,
A sunbeam on the saddened lawn
I smile, and weep to be withdrawn
In early years.

"Thy leaves will come! but songful spring
Will see no leaf of mine;
Her bells will ring, her bride's-maids sing
When my young leaves are withering
Where no suns shine.

"O might I breathe morn's dewy breath,
When June's sweet Sabbath's chime!
But, thine before my time, O Death!
I go where no flower blossometh,
Before my time.

"Even as the blushes of the morn
Vanish, and long ere noon
The dew-drop dieth on the thorn,
So fair I bloomed; and was I born
To die as soon?

"To love my mother and to die —
To perish in my bloom!
Is this my sad brief history? —
A tear dropped from a mother's eye
Into the tomb.

"He lived and loved — will sorrow say —
By early sorrow tried;
He smiled, he sighed, he past away;
His life was but an April day —
He loved and died!

"My mother smiles, then turns away,
But turns away to weep;
They whisper round me — what they say
I need not hear, for in the clay
I soon must sleep.

"Oh, love is sorrow! sad it is
To be both tried and true!
I ever trembled in my bliss;
Now there are farewells in a kiss —
They sigh adieu.

"But woodbines flaunt when bluebells fade,
Where Don reflects the skies;
And many a youth in Shire-cliffs' shade
Will ramble where my boyhood played,
Though Alfred dies.

"Then panting woods the breeze will feel,
And bowers, as heretofore,
Beneath their load of roses reel;
But I through woodbined lanes shall steal
No more, no more.

"Well, lay me by my brother's side,
Where late we stood and wept;
For I was stricken when he died —
I felt the arrow as he sighed
His last and slept."

I find that I could, did I follow my inclination, make a volume, and not an essay, by mere extracts; but I must deny my desire, and close with two short poems, which paint in glowing words the author's own character and genius.

A POET.

"Child of the Hopeless! two hearts broke
  When thou wast orphan'd here:
They left a treasure in thy breast,
  The soul of Pity's tear.
And thou must be — not what thou wilt; —
  Say then, what would'st thou be?
'A Poet!' Oh, if thou would'st steep
  Deep thoughts in ecstasy,

"Nor poet of the rich be thou,
  Nor poet of the poor;
Nor harper of the swarming town,
  Nor minstrel of the moor;
But be the bard of all mankind,
  The prophet of all time,
And tempt the saints in heaven to steal
  Earth's truth-created rhyme.

"Be the Columbus of a world
  Where wisdom knows not fear;
The Homer of a race of men
  Who need not sword and spear.

God in thy heart, and God in thee,
  If thou to men canst show,
Thou makest mortals angels here,
  Their home a heaven below.

" Upon a rock thou sett'st thy feet,
  And callest Death thy slave:
'Here lies a man!' Eternity
  Shall write upon thy grave;
'A Bard lies here! — O softly tread,
  Ye never-wearied years!
And bless, O World, a memory
  Immortal as thy tears!'"

A POET'S EPITAPH.

" Stop, Mortal! Here thy brother lies,
  The Poet of the Poor.
His books were rivers, woods, and skies,
  The meadow, and the moor;
His teachers were the torn hearts' wail,
  The tyrant, and the slave,
The street, the factory, the jail,
  The palace — and the grave!
The meanest thing, earth's feeblest worm,
  He feared to scorn or hate;
And honor'd in a peasant's form
  The equal of the great.

But if he lov'd the rich who make
  The poor man's little more,
Ill could he praise the rich who take
  From plunder'd labor's store.
A hand to do, a head to plan,
  A heart to feel and dare —
Tell man's worst foes, here lies the man
  Who drew them as they are."

The battle for labor has been manfully carried on; and the battle for labor has been a battle for freedom. Every gain to the rights of industry has been equally a gain to the rights of liberty. The franchise of toil has advanced the franchise of thought; and the independence of handicraft has extended the independence of humanity. The man of privilege is the man of the Past; the man of labor is the man of the Future. The man of the Future, even in England, gains on the man of the Past; but the man of the Past, though enfeebled, is not destroyed, and it is not desirable that he should be. He is a portion of the national memory, and he is worthy of existence as an agent in national civilization. As yet he has had no reason to complain. He still stands upon dark and massive battlements, and proudly unfurls the banner which was won at Cressy or Agincourt. Commerce, however, has stripped forests from his hills, to spread mightier forests on the sea;

his flag is obscured in the smoke of increasing manufactures, and the music of his halls grows faint in the din of surrounding looms and hammers.

The social changes of England have been anticipated by no extended foresight, and they have been met by no adequate preparation. The external greatness of the country has been enlarged, but the poor man's comforts have been diminished; and this wretchedness the poor man endures under the heavy aggravation of most painful contrast. His lair is in the midst of palaces; his empty basket is surrounded by luxury, which earth is exhausted to supply; he faints by the odor of feasts upon his weakness, as he passes by the halls of banqueting, and his squalid rags are spurned by the pampered menial that shrinks from him in the street. And why, he asks himself, is this? Why, with honesty and hands, have I not at least leave to toil? When toil is given me, why have I not leave to live? Because my hands have been manacled by restrictive legislation; because idleness has become necessity, and starvation, law; because my wages have been swallowed in maintaining privilege; because debts, which cause nations to stand aghast, have been contracted to pay the mercenaries of foreign despots. This money has but sold my days to hopeless servitude; and the victories of my brave compatriots have given nothing to me and to my children, but an everlasting inheritance of hunger.

The statesmen of England have been wanting in the grand sagacity which a mighty country in extraordinary times demanded. The manufacturing power of England has in half a century grown to a hugeness unexampled in the history of trade ; but nothing comparatively was done in reference to this immense revolution. While squires declaimed in Parliament on the iniquity of poaching, and called for rigid laws to save partridges from the infamy of being shot by plebeian gunpowder, — while ministers taxed the country for millions, to place one fool on a rickety throne, instead of another, — masses of human beings were silently conglomerating within limited districts, forming a dense and a peculiar population. Who were those, let us ask, who constituted this population ? They were families, who, leaving their cabins behind them in the wilds of Ireland, sought to escape famine in the country, and found it in the city. They were families, who, streaming down from Welsh and Scottish mountains, were tempted from their cloudy solitudes to pursue fortune in strange crowds, and met with hardships which their sterile hills had never threatened. They were families from the green dells and quiet hamlets of England, whom high rents and bad times had scourged from the open light of nature to the filthy cellars of the smoky town. Collected thus from various districts, by similar distress, they had nothing in common but ignorance and want. Once involved in factory labor, their condition was destiny. They had no other refuge on which to fall back ; live they might, while work was for them, and when it failed, they must be paupers, or they must die. From the plough to the cotton mill, was like the passage to the grave ; it could be made but once, and could never be retraced.

Here, then, a distinctive class was incorporated with the nation ; and this class had distinctive wants. What had been done for these people ? Did each person bring from his native district a decent education, with which his native district had supplied him ? No provision existed for any such supply. Armies abounded for the peninsula of Europe and the peninsula of India, but schoolmasters were scarce for the cottages of Ireland and the cottages of Britain. With solemn cathedrals, and venerable colleges, with triumph of arms, and conquest of empires, England has allowed generations of her children to live and die in a most forlorn ignorance ; with vast revenues for state, for nobles, for hierarchies, she has nothing to spare for the souls of the poor. Would it be wonderful, then, if masses, thus goaded for mere existence, thus neglected, should start up in the madness of their want and the fury of their passions, and stain their age with deeds which history would shudder to record? But no. Gloriously they have borne misfortune; patiently they have endured injustice; valiantly, wisely, and humanely they will redress their wrongs.

There is hope for the toilsmen of England! Yes; but where? In themselves; not in peers and princes, not in parties or statesmen; but in their own stout hearts, in their own enlightened exertions, in their own moral and intellectual exaltation. The virtuous cannot be despised, and the wise cannot be conquered; and no one can doubt, who has watched the progress of events, that, within a few years, virtue and wisdom have made progress among the operatives of Britain. Thousands and thousands have passed blamelessly through suffering, which in other times would have had the praise of martyrdom. Imprisoned men, forgetting all vindictive feeling, have used their hours of confinement to send forth instruction to their brothers clad in noble diction, and breathing a high philosophy. Humble men from the Chartist ranks, dragged to jail for sedition, have shown their power for such lofty, intellectual, and moral achievement. Let English toilsmen take courage; ay, and English toilswomen also.

Have we not evidence of graceful and elegant attainment in this country among a laboring class of the fair sex; evidence, that heads are not idle, while hands are busy? American factory girls, with a vivacity of mind which no fatigue can depress, have added to our literature; and their contributions are distinguished by an excellence of thought which needs but small indulgence from the critical, and by a purity of sentiment which merits all the praises of the good.

Let this voice from the heart of toiling womanhood go from the girls of America, and fall upon the weary spirits of their British sisters; and let it come back across the wild Atlantic in joyous echoes of exulting hope. The daughters of labor, even in England, may not despair of redemption. The sons of labor can gain it for themselves, and help their weaker companions. They have many examples and predecessors; kingly men, from plough and hammer, from hill-side and dyke. An era, I would fain believe, is coming for the English toilsman, when his labor will purchase him more than a living death; when an existence will be fairly within his reach, which will include whatever confers pure enjoyment and moral elevation; he will then be sustained in his own self-respect. He will not be ashamed of a virtuous calling; and none will dare to regard his position with contempt; no dastard blush will suffuse the brow which has been wrinkled by the care of a hard but honest occupation; and the hand will seek no concealment, which has been roughened by industry, but has never been soiled by corruption. Under any circumstances, in any state of things, in any country, if we appreciate truth and reality; if we are not cheated by sham, and glare, and vanity; if we are not deceived by gaud and shadow, — the fustian which covers an upright soul is a garb of honor; and that is the most kingly sheen which clothes the most kingly worth.

OLIVER GOLDSMITH.

OLIVER GOLDSMITH was born November 10, 1728, in Pallas, County of Longford, Ireland. Other places contend for the honor of his birth, but this has the claim of authority. His father was a clergyman, with a numerous family and slender means; with no faculty of economy, and a strong desire for expenditure. It is needless to dwell minutely on a life so well known as Goldsmith's, or one that may so easily be known. His childhood had some eccentricities, and his college career was marked by a few rows and freaks; but with all his wildness, his writings show that the kind heart of his childhood continued fresh to the end, and that his college experience left him, at least, classical knowledge and classical tastes. Having been a medical student in Edinburgh and Leyden, then he became a pennyless wanderer on the continent of Europe; after piping to peasants and spouting in convents, he returned to London, and there he began as a drudge to pedagogues, and ended as a drudge to publishers. The amount of desultory composition on every topic, which, for years, he furnished to his employers, must excite our wonder ; but that which most excites it, is the general beauty which distinguishes these compositions, and the pittance by which they were recompensed. Herein, however, was the consolation of his privacy. He was just to his own powers ; he gratified his own fine taste ; labor was mitigated by an inward sense of dignity ; and he was saved from that weight of lassitude, which presses upon no hireling with so deadly an influence, as upon the hireling of literature. At last, he toiled his way to fame ; but his expenditure outran his prosperity. Accustomed, hitherto, to small sums, moderate ones seemed exhaustless, and on this delusion of a poor man, unacquainted with money and the world, he acted.

Always thoughtless, he now became lavish ; he not only spent his money, but anticipated work ; he not only emptied his purse, but he drew extravagantly on his faculties. He was in arrears with his publishers for books, not finished, even for books to be written. With much to pay, and nothing to receive ; with difficulties pressing on the mental power, which was required in its utmost vigor to remove them ; his life was approaching to a crisis. A fever, rendered fatal by distress of mind, and by his own injudicious treatment, carried him off in the forty-sixth year of his age. Dr. Johnson, who did not often expose his sensibility, was extremely moved; and Edmund Burke burst into tears. It was computed that his debts, when he died, amounted to two thousand pounds, upon which Dr. Johnson exclaims, in a letter to Boswell, "Was poet ever so trusted before?" So loved, indeed, was Goldsmith, that the tradesmen, to whom part of this was due, murmured no complaint; put no stain upon his memory; but following departed genius with thoughts of charity, their affectionate observation was, that, if he had lived, he would have paid them all. Ay! if he had lived! if he had lived, he would have paid them all; and how much, too, would he have given to the world, in addition to that obligation which the world never discharged! The greater part of the debt which encumbered the last days of his earthly existence, was one for which booksellers held a mortgage upon his mind. To many of these men, his mind was a fountain of wealth; and to us, it is a fountain of instruction and enjoyment. Contemporaries gave Goldsmith a tomb; his most venerable companion gave him an epitaph; posterity have given him their hearts. Few can see the tomb; few can understand the language of the epitaph ; but millions love his genius, and in the memory of their living affections, they enshrine his name.

After all, his fate was not worse than others in his class. No man heard where, or cared how, Chatterton groaned away his soul ; so his heart broke in agony, and no Bristol trader inquired about the unhappy but inspired boy, who, perhaps, grew up beside his threshold. Chatterton knew nothing of the market or the stocks, and nobody listened to him, and nobody cared for him, and nobody heard him. He was alone ; his brother was not near him ; his sister knew not of the despair that gathered upon his sinking heart. He looked around him, and all was gloomy, all was dismal. He did not wait for starvation to do its worst ; but, ere it could come to wither and to kill him, from some process, easy as that of a bare bodkin, he sought his last and long quietus ; and where he sought, he found it.

The character of Goldsmith, is one which does not tax analysis ; it is felt by instinct ; and that happy phrase, " good natured," defines it with a singular accuracy. Goldsmith's good nature, though it exhausted his purse, did not exhaust itself. It was an unfailing well-spring ; it was ever pure and fresh, bubbling from a copious fountain of kindness, and refreshing life around him with streams of gayety, of fondness, and of pity. There was a benignity in him which gave his heart an interest in the humblest creature. Early in life, in writing home, he says, "if there be a favorite dog in the family, let me be remembered to him." His attachment to children was as strong as it was amiable. The younger Colman speaks in rapture of his acquaintance with Goldsmith, when in infant insolence he used to tweak the poet's nose ; and the poet, in return, played thimble-rig with the child. Nor was this merely deference to the son of a rich man and a critic. Goldsmith was an idol, also, to the children of the poor ; it was his common practice to go among them with pockets full of gingerbread, and to set them dancing to the sound of his flute. His, in every scene, was a simple nature ; and he around whom rustics pranced on the banks of the Loire, was the same around whom ragged innocents gabbled and rejoiced in the garrets of Old Bailey. Goldsmith's humanity to the poor, generally, was most courteous and most bountiful. His charity would often have been sublime, if the improvidence of his temper did not drive him to contrivances to supply it, which gave it an air of the ludicrous. One morning towards the close of his college course, a cousin and fellow-student of his knocked at the door of his chamber. No reply. He knocked again. Still no reply. He then broke it open. Goldsmith was in bed, literally *in* it, for he was stuck bodily into the feathers. Some poor woman had told him a tragical story ; he was out of money, so he brought her to the college, and gave her his blankets.

Let me take another instance from his later life, an instance which, as I think, is most characteristic of the author and the man. Suppose ourselves gazing into a humble chamber, in the humblest part of London. A ragged bed is in one corner, a broken wash-stand is in another. A crazy table is placed near a small dusty window, and a man sits by this table on the only chair which the room contains. The stature of the man is short, and his face is pale ; his position has an air of thought, and his look, the glow of fancy. This man, whose forehead is bulging out with sentiments and ideas so as to defy all rules of sculpture, is ugly ; but he is ugly only to those who cannot see the light of the spirit through the shrine of the countenance. To those who know the touch of nature that makes all men akin, he is inexpressibly dear ; and they love to gaze on his homely portrait, as if it were lovely as ever dawned upon a sculptor's dream. The man is Oliver Goldsmith, and as we now describe him, he is engaged in writing his Essay on the State of Polite Learning in Europe. A knock at his lowly door arouses him, and a visitor enters.

The visitor is Bishop Percy, the admirable collector of Reliques of Ancient English Poetry. Goldsmith courteously gives the prelate his only chair, and takes himself a seat upon the window-sill. They are engaged in an earnest conversation on belles-lettres and the fine arts, when a ragged but decent little girl comes into the room, and with a respectful obeisance to Goldsmith, says, " My mamma sends her compliments, sir, and begs the favor of you to lend her a pot of coals."

As Goldsmith's fortunes increased, so did his gifts to the poor, and food was added to fuel. After he had entertained a large party at breakfast, he distributed the fragments among a few poor women whom he had kept waiting for the purpose. A vulgar guest remarked, that he must be very rich to afford such bounty. " It is not wealth, my dear sir," said Goldsmith, " it is inclination ; I have only to suppose that a few more friends have been of the party, and then it amounts to the same thing." He was, besides, always surrounded by a circle of needy writers, whom he had not the firmness to refuse, nor the prudence to discharge. He was also beset by destitute countrymen, who found a ready way to his last shilling, through his compassion and his patriotism. To such people, bounty was no virtue, but with Goldsmith, pity gave ere charity began ; and charity had always the start of wisdom. Much as there was in such actions which implied want of purpose and want of thought; there was goodness, too, upon which no tone of distress ever fell in vain. "He has been known," says Prior, the most genial of his biographers, "to quit his bed at night, and even when laboring under indisposition, in order to relieve the miserable, and when money was scarce, or, to be procured with difficulty by borrowing, he has, nevertheless, shared it with such as presented any claims to charity.

"At an evening party of friends, he once threw down his cards, and rushed from the room, and when asked the cause, on his return, of such an abrupt retreat, 'I could not bear,' said he, 'to hear that unfortunate woman in the street, half singing, half sobbing; for such tones could only arise from the extremity of distress; her voice grated painfully on my ear, so that I could not rest until I had sent her away.' To the unfortunate, even to those made so by their own errors, he ever turned with the spirit of a good Samaritan; and when he had relieved them with his money, he pleaded for them with his pen. His word was ever for the feeble, the oppressed, and the unhappy; and passages of pathetic eloquence abound in his writings, which nothing could have inspired, but the finest natural feeling. 'Who are those,' he exclaims, in the

character of his citizen of the world, 'who make the streets their couch, and find a short repose from wretchedness at the doors of the opulent? These are strangers, wanderers, orphans, whose circumstances are too humble to expect redress, and whose distresses are too great even for pity. Their wretchedness excites rather horror than compassion. Some are without the covering even of rags, and others emaciated with disease. The world has disclaimed them; society turns its back upon their distress, and has given them up to nakedness and hunger. . . . . .
Poor houseless creatures! the world will give you reproaches, but will not give you relief. The slightest misfortunes of the great, the most imaginary uneasiness of the rich, are aggravated with all the power of eloquence, and are held up to engage our attention and sympathetic sorrow. The poor weep unheeded, persecuted by every species of petty tyranny, and every law which gives others a security becomes an enemy to them.' "

This generosity of temper, united with keen observation, enabled Goldsmith to pierce readily through the disguises of selfishness; so that, with his comic sagacity, and his genial perception of the ludicrous, no writer can give more amusing pictures, than he does, of sordid follies. Even in his very youth, we have the narrative of an adventure, which promises all the thoughtful drollery that he afterwards exhibited. He had gone in a freak to Cork, mounted on a noble horse, and with thirty pounds in his pocket. It was not long, ere he was returning, with merely five shillings, and mounted on an animal which he called Fiddle-back. He was, however, blithe and careless, for near to the city there was a college friend, who had often pressed him to a visit. "We shall enjoy," he would say, "both the city and the country; and you shall command my stable and my purse."

Going towards his friend's house, he divided his five shillings with a destitute woman, and on his arrival, he found his friend an invalid; but so cordial was his reception, that remorse struck him for not having given the whole five shillings to his needy sister. He stated his case, and opened his heart to his friend. His friend walked to and fro, rubbed his hands, and Goldsmith attributed this to the force of his compassion, which required motion, and to the delicacy of his sentiments, which commanded silence. The hour was growing late, and Goldsmith's appetite had been long at craving point. "At length an old woman came into the room with two plates, one spoon, and a dirty cloth, which she laid upon the table. This appearance," says Goldsmith, "without increasing my spirits, did not diminish my appetite. My protectress soon returned with one bowl of sago, a small porringer of sour milk, a loaf of stale brown bread, and the heel of an old cheese. My friend," continues the poet, " apologized, that his illness obliged him to live on slops, and that better fare was not in the house ; observing, at the same time, that a milk diet was certainly the most healthful. At eight o'clock he again recommended a regular life, declaring that, for his part, he would lie down with the lamb, and rise with the lark. My hunger was at this time so exceedingly sharp, that I wished for another slice of the loaf, but was obliged to go to bed without even that refreshment."

Next morning Goldsmith spoke of his departure. " To be sure," said this munificent friend, " the longer you stay away from your mother, the more you will grieve her, and your other relatives ; and possibly they are already afflicted at hearing of this foolish expedition you have made." Goldsmith, then reminding him of former good turns, tried to borrow a guinea from him. " Why look you, Mr. Goldsmith," said Solomon the younger, " I have paid you all you ever lent me, and this sickness of mine has left me bare of cash. But, I have bethought myself of a conveyance for you. Sell your horse, and I will furnish you with a much better one to ride on." I readily, said Goldsmith, grasped at this proposal, and begged to see the nag; on which he led me to his bed-chamber, and from under the bed pulled out a stout oak stick. "Here," said he, "take this in your hand, and it will carry you to your mother's with more safety than such a horse as you ride." Goldsmith was about to lay it on his back, but a casual visitor coming in, his generous friend introduced him with eulogium and with enthusiasm. Both of them had an invitation to dinner; for which Goldsmith was quite prepared; and it seemed not less acceptable to the amiable invalid. At the close of the evening, the entertainer offered Goldsmith a bed, who then told his former host to go home and take care of his excellent horse, but that he would never enter his house again.

The objections against Goldsmith's benevolence of character, drawn from Boswell, are easily answered. Boswell did not like Goldsmith. He did not, and could not, do him justice. The position of Goldsmith near Johnson, was galling to Boswell. He was humiliated when Goldsmith was present; for, familiar as Boswell was with the great moralist, his relation to him was not like that of the poet, an equal and a brother. The conviction of such inferiority was intolerable to a man of Boswell's temper; and the sternness with which Johnson put to silence every effort of his to depreciate Goldsmith, so sharpened his asperity, that occasionally it seems half malignant. Whatever foibles belonged to Oliver Goldsmith, no one could be ignorant that the author of "The Traveller" was a man of genius; and the very dignity in which Johnson held the profession of letters, would never permit him, even if affection did not interfere, to treat Goldsmith with irreverence. If for a moment, in his turbulent dogmatism, he forgot the respect which was a brother's due, an immediate and complete apology expressed his contrition, and changed him from the superior to the suppliant.

It was a hard lot to Boswell, that, notwithstanding all his assiduity, Goldsmith maintained a communion with Johnson, to which he could never dare. Boswell's situation was that of a petted favorite, a pleasant amanuensis, a lackey to the mind; but the place of Goldsmith was that of prince with prince. Goldsmith took little notice of Boswell, not from any special feeling, I apprehend, but because there was nothing in him that struck his fancy; and Boswell, like all favorites, insolent, was mortally chagrined, that one whom he would fain consider beneath him, should so quietly but so effectually show him that he was merely a subordinate. The impression of Goldsmith which Boswell's remarks tend to leave, is, that he had not only a vanity which was disgusting, but an envy which was detestable. But Prior, who has sifted all the facts, exposes successfully the absurdity of the charges. Boswell, himself, was a man both vain and envious; and such a man is always the most likely to charge vanity and envy on another. Goldsmith unquestionably had vanity, a vanity which, added to a grotesque appearance and ungainly manners, became a ludicrous oddity, and, as in the case of every kind-hearted person of confiding simplicity and open speech, he was at the mercy of his critics. He had all the youthfulness of genius. Necessity compelled him to severe exertion. In the hours of relaxation he gambolled as a boy, and capered in every whim which his guileless and unsuspicious temper prompted. Much he said and did in sheer sportiveness, which Boswell has set down seriously, if not in malice.

Goldsmith had vanity that was undisguised, but it had the association of goodness to save it from offending, and of genius to shield it from derision. Boswell, who ridicules the vanity of Goldsmith, had also a vanity of his own, but, sooth to say, it was of a very odd kind; it was the vanity of servitude, the vanity of voluntary abasement, the vanity that seemed paradoxically to combine the mean and the heroic; a meanness that first submitted to abuse, and a heroism that afterwards recorded it ; a vanity, which had strong resemblance to that ascribed by Dean Swift to " John," in " The Tale of the Tub ; " the vanity, allow me to speak it in the vernacular Saxon, the vanity of being kicked. I do not, however, deny that Boswell has left us a most fascinating book, a book which he could not perhaps have written, had his mind been of an order more aspiring and more independent.

I have confined my remarks chiefly to a distinctive quality in the character of Goldsmith, universally conceded ; but his whole worth was by no means confined to this. No gross vices are recorded against him ; his general habits appear to have been comparatively unstained ; his general tastes were simple ; he was temperate almost to abstinence ; and excess he regarded with abhorrence. To speak thus is to speak negatively, but these negatives, connected with Goldsmith's position and his times, have a value that is positive. But one virtue eminently positive, belongs to Goldsmith, and that is, his exceeding literary purity ; the sacred independence with which he used his talents, and the sacred purposes to which he applied them. Follies were his, which gathered afflictions about his lot, that not all his innocent hilarity could throw off. Carelessness brought misfortunes upon him, which broke at last his elastic capacity of endurance ; but no destitution was ever a temptation to his literary conscience, and no pressure ever bent its rectitude. From the beginning, Goldsmith eschewed patrons; he acted, from the first, on the manly resolution of seeking support in the honest exertion of his own powers. The Earl of Northumberland, going as Lord Lieutenant to Ireland, offered him assistance; Goldsmith declined for himself, and only requested protection for his brother, a worthy pastor and a worthy man. Sir John Hawkins calls him a fool; but his own words show he was as wise as he was conscientious: "I have," said he, "no dependence on the promises of the great men. I look to the booksellers for support; they are my best friends."

It is true, that Goldsmith could not always have an end equal to his genius; but he never perjured his convictions, nor bartered his soul. It is true, that his main object was often merely to do a certain quantity of work, and receive a certain sum of wages, and of this he sometimes complains with a sort of melancholy pleasantry. He says, in reference to his History of England, "I have been a good deal abused lately in the newspapers for betraying the liberty of the people. God knows, I had no thought for or against liberty in my head; my whole aim being to make a book of a decent size, that as Squire Richard says, would do no harm to nobody." But though Goldsmith had often to think more of sustenance than fame, he merely wrote rapidly, he did not write falsely. Living in an age, when a name sold a book, and when patrons made a name, and when dedications earned patrons, Goldsmith passed over titles and gratified his affections: the first of his poems he inscribed to an indigent brother, and the others he inscribed to his immediate friends.

He was ever perplexed with debts and surrounded with difficulties: his heart always craving for money to give, and his supply always far behind his craving, yet he could reject propositions which men, who have secured a reputation for more austere virtue than Goldsmith, would have found elegant excuses for accepting. The British Cabinet, by a confidential agent, intimated a munificent remuneration for his pen. The poet occupied sordid chambers, and labored like a slave; but here was his answer: "I can earn as much as will supply my wants without writing for any party; the assistance therefore, which you offer is unnecessary to me."

Can you think of a much stronger temptation among earthly struggles, than the offer of a rich government to a poor writer? Judge Goldsmith, then, by the severity of his trial, and give him the credit of his victory. But he was honest with the public as he was with patrons. Needy though he was, he sought the suffrage of men only by means which tended to make them wiser, and to make them better; and of those compositions which multitudes seek, as much as they should shun them, and which it is as easy as it is dishonorable to produce, not one can be laid to the charge of Goldsmith. The spirit of his works is as chaste, as their style is classical; and to him belongs the glory, of having purified expression, when the phraseology even of women was coarse; and of having consecrated the novel to virtue, when the pen of fiction was dipped in the offscourings of passion.

I am compelled to pass from a brief review of Goldsmith's character, to an equally brief review of his writings. The writings of Goldsmith, if they had no other excellence, would be remarkable for their felicitous versatility. The author is successively presented to us as historian, essayist, dramatist, poët, and novelist. The few words I can say of Goldsmith, as a writer, will take the order which I have now indicated.

As a historian, Goldsmith accomplishes all at which he aims. He does not promise much, but he does more than he promises. He takes, it is true, facts which had been already collected, but he shapes them with an art that is all his own. He has the rare faculty of being brief without being dry; of being at once perspicuous and compressed, and of giving to the merest abridgment the interest of dramatic illusion. Doctor Johnson set a high value on Goldsmith, if not as a historian, at least as a narrator; and Dr. Johnson was a man, whose critical austerity even friendship rarely softened. Dr Johnson went so far, as to place Goldsmith above Robertson. When we have taken into consideration Johnson's prejudices against Robertson for being a Scotchman and a Presbyterian, a worth will still remain in the opinion, which we must allow to Goldsmith. Robertson, Johnson represents as crushed under his own weight; or as like a man that packs gold in wool, the wool taking more room than the gold. Goldsmith, he says, puts into his book as much as his book will hold. No man, he asserts, will read Robertson's cumbrous detail a second time; but Goldsmith's plain narrative will please again and again. Johnson remarked of Goldsmith in one of his conversations, — "He is now writing a Natural History, and he will make it as entertaining as a Persian Tale." With these histories of Goldsmith we cannot dispense; a beautiful mixture of the agreeable and the useful, they are dear to us with all their imperfections; they are lessons for our childhood, and relaxation for our maturity. They have a permanent existence in our literature, and they deserve it. They deserve it, not alone for their charms of expression, but for qualities of higher worth; for purity of sentiment, for honesty of purpose, for benevolence of heart, for the wisdom of a liberal spirit, and the moderation of a humane temper.

As an essayist, Goldsmith ranks with the highest in our language. With a keen observation of life and manners, he unites delightful ease; and he softens caustic sarcasm with a pleasant humor. Amidst a varied experience, he preserved a simple heart; and he drew human nature as he found it, with the freedom of a satirist, but never with the coldness of a cynic. The essays of Goldsmith are wise as well as amusing, and display as much sagacity as variety. They abound in impressive moral teachings, in apt examples, and in beautiful illustrations. Serious, when soberness is wisdom, and gay when laughter is not folly; they can prompt the smile, they can also start the tear; inspiration comes with the occasion, in unexpected eloquence, and in unbidden pathos.

To speak of Goldsmith as an essayist, is to suggest a comparison of his merits with writers whose excellence in didactic and humorous composition forms an elevated and a severe standard. But Goldsmith will bear the comparison. He has not, indeed, the undefinable grace of Addison; nor the solemn wisdom of Johnson. But neither has Addison his freshness, his hearty and broad ridicule, the cheerful comicry which will not be satisfied with an elegant simper, but must have the loud and open laugh. Johnson on the solemn themes of humanity maintains a melancholy grandeur; he sits in despondency and solitude; his general reflections on life and destiny are the deep sighings of a heart that seeks for hope, but has not found it; the pantings of a troubled soul alarmed by superstition, but wanting faith; they are lofty, but cheerless; they are eloquent, but monotonous; they have music, but it is the music of lamentation; they are the modulations of a dirge. Johnson knew well the dark abstractions which belong to our nature; but he did not understand the details of common existence as Goldsmith did. He could moralize, but he could not paint; he has splendid passages, but no pictures; he could philosophize, but he could not create. He has, therefore, left us no special individualities, to which our fancies can give local habitations; he has made no addition to that world of beings, whose population and whose history belong to imagination; he has given it no new inhabitant, none to walk beside the "Vicar of Wakefield," or "Sir Roger de Coverly." As for "Rasselas," he is a declamatory shadow; and cloud-formed as he is, the vapor does not long preserve a shape; for the outlines soon melt into the illimitable expanse of gloomy meditation.

After reading a paper in the "Rambler," or a chapter in "Rasselas," I take up Goldsmith's "Citizen of the World" with a new relish; and when I have perused some pages, I feel resuscitated from depression by its satire, its shrewdness, its pleasantry, and good sense. What a pungent impersonation of poverty and folly is Beau Tibbs, such an admirable combination of the dandy and the loafer. Johnson could have no more conceived of Beau Tibbs, than he could have invented a dialect for little fishes. Goldsmith at one time told the critic, that if he gave little fishes language, that he would make little fishes speak like whales. So he would make Beau Tibbs speak like "The Last Man." But Goldsmith understood what little fishes should say, if they had the gift of speech; it is no wonder, that he knew the proper phraseology of Beau Tibbs, who had that gift with a most miraculous fluency.

Beau Tibbs is a perfect character of the Jeremy Diddler school. Dressed in the finery of rag-fair, he talks of the balls and assemblies he attends. He has invitations to noblemen's feasts for a month to come; yet he jumps at an offer to share a mug of porter; he bets a thousand guineas, and in the same breath, it is "Dear Drybone, lend me half-a-crown for a minute or two." Once in company with his Chinese friend, the Citizen of the World, they are asked twenty pounds for a seat to see the coronation. The Chinese sage inquires, whether a coronation will clothe, or feed, or fatten him. "Sir," replied the man, "you seem to be under a mistake; all you can bring away is the pleasure of having it to say, that you saw the coronation." "Blast me," cries Tibbs, "if that be all, there is no need of paying for that, since I am resolved to have that pleasure, whether I am there or not."

Beau Tibbs, then, is a character, and so is the "Man in Black." Where will you find more originality? A most delightful compound is the "Man in Black;" a rarity not to be met with often; a true oddity, with the tongue of Timon, and the heart of Uncle Toby. He proclaims war against pauperism, yet he cannot say "no" to a beggar. He ridicules generosity, yet would he share with the poor whatever he possessed. He glories in having become a niggard, as he wishes to be thought, and thus describes his conversion. Having told how he quitted the folly of liberality, "I now," said he, "pursuing a course of uninterrupted frugality, seldom wanted a dinner, and was consequently invited to twenty. I soon began to get the character of a saving hunks, that had money, and insensibly I grew into esteem. Neighbors have asked my advice in the disposal of their daughters, and

I have always taken care not to give any. I have contracted a friendship with an alderman only by observing, that if we take a farthing from a thousand pounds, it will be a thousand pounds no longer. I have been invited to a pawn-broker's table by pretending to hate gravy, and am now actually on a treaty of marriage with a rich widow, for only having observed that bread was rising. If ever I am asked a question, whether I know it or not, instead of answering it, I only smile, and look wise. If a charity is proposed, I go about with the hat, but put nothing in myself. If a wretch solicits my pity, I observe that the world is filled with impostors, and take a certain method of not being deceived by never relieving."

As a dramatist, Goldsmith is amusing; and if to excite laughter be, as Johnson asserts it is, the chief end of comedy, Goldsmith attains it. His plots, however, are extravagant, and his personages are oddities rather than characters. Goldsmith's plays want the contrivance which belongs to highest art; but they have all those ingenious accidents which are suitable for stage effect. They are, in fact, deficient in that insight, which pertains only to great dramatic genius. "The Good-natured Man" is an agreeable satire on the follies of benevolence, and "She stoops to Conquer," a laughable burlesque on a very improbable mistake.

Croaker, in the one, is an effective caricature on men of groaning and long faces; and Tony Lumpkin, in the other, is a broad, grinning stereotype of a foolish mother's fool. These two comedies comprise all Goldsmith's theatrical writings. Both of them abound in drollery and strong touches of nature; but they do not give the author an exalted position among dramatists, and they do not promise that he could have reached it.

In referring to Goldsmith as a poet, I have no intention to commit the impertinence of formal criticism. I have an easy and a pleasant work. I have nothing to defend, and nothing to refute. I have only to call up simple recollections, which are endeared to us all by the unanimous experience of a common pleasure. Who has not read "The Traveller," and "The Deserted Village," and "The Hermit," and "Retaliation?" And who that has read them will forget, or not recall them, as among the sweetest melodies which his thoughts preserve? "The Traveller" has the most ambitious aim of Goldsmith's poetical compositions. The author, placed on a height of the Alps, muses and moralizes on the countries around him. His object, it appears, is to show the equality of happiness, which consists with diversities of circumstances and situations. The poem is, therefore, mainly didactic. Description and reflection are subservient to an ethical purpose, and this purpose is never left out of sight. The descriptive passages are all vivid, but some of them are imperfect. Italy, for instance, in its prominent aspects, is boldly sketched. We are transported to the midst of its mountains, woods, and temples; we are under its sunny skies, we are embosomed in its fruits and flowers, we breathe its fragrant air, and we are charmed by its matchless landscapes; but we miss the influence of its arts, and the solemn impression of its former grandeur. We are made to survey a nation in degeneracy and decay; but we are not relieved by the glow of Raffael, or excited by the might of the Colosseum.

The fact is, that Goldsmith, with a pure taste and a sweet fancy, was not a man of varied culture, or of wide reflection. The general equality, the honest toil, the frugal habits, the domestic virtue, and the heroic patriotism of the Swiss, are eloquently commended. But of all countries on the European continent, France was the one of Goldsmith's affections, and his experience in that gay land is detailed with the partiality of a lover. The character of the Hollanders has the most severity; that of the English the most power. Whether Goldsmith's description of the English be considered true or false, none can deny the force of its expression:

"Stern o'er each bosom, reason holds her state,
With daring aims irregularly great;
Pride in their port, defiance in their eye,
I see the lords of human kind pass by;
Intent on high designs, a thoughtful band,
By forms unfashioned, fresh from nature's hand;
Fierce in their native hardihood of soul,
True to imagined right, above control;
While e'en the peasant boasts these rights to scan,
And learns to venerate himself as man."

"The Deserted Village" belongs to the heart, and the heart guards it from the profanation of analysis. It is a poem upon which the heart has long decided. Each of us might say, with the author of that Sweet Auburn which he has immortalized:

"How often have I loitered o'er thy green,
Where humble happiness endeared each scene;
How often have I paused on every charm,
The sheltered cot, the cultivated farm,
The never failing brook, the busy mill,
The silent church, that topped the neighboring hill,
The hawthorn bush, with seats beneath the shade
For talking age, and whispering lovers made."

The characters of this poem are our household friends, angels whom we love to entertain, yet not as strangers, nor unawares. Their names were on our lips at school, and they will be pleasant to the grave. Who of us will not ever reverence the Village Pastor? Who of us have not been guests in his chimney corner, and listened with him to the aged beggar and the broken soldier?

"The broken soldier kindly bade to stay,
Sat by the fire, and talked the night away;
Wept o'er his wounds, and tales of sorrow done,
Shouldered his crutch, and showed how fields were won."

We have all, too, followed this good man to the House of Prayer, where he shone with unaffected grace, where the young loved him, and where the old admired; we have followed him to the house of mourning, where his steps were soft as mercy, and where his tones were filled with heaven:

"Beside the bed, where parting life was laid,
And sorrow, guilt, and pain by turns dismayed,
The reverend champion stood; at his control
Despair and anguish fled the struggling soul;
Comfort came down, the trembling wretch to raise,
And his last faltering accents whispered praise."

Nor is the good old Schoolmaster less a favorite with us; for

"He was kind, or if severe in aught,
The love he bore to learning was in fault;

The village wondered all, how much he knew,
'T was certain he could write, and cipher too;
Lands he could measure, terms and tides presage,
And e'en the story ran that he could gauge.
In arguing, too, the parson owned his skill,
For e'en though vanquished, he could argue still:
While words of learned length and thundering sound
Amazed the gazing rustics ranged around;
And still they gazed, and still the wonder grew
That one small head could carry all he knew."

Goldsmith deserves his popularity, for he loved the people; it was mankind he respected, and not office. In many ways he was not unlike Burns, but most like him in personal independence and popular sympathy. Burns, with all his impassioned aspiration, has nothing finer than this:

"Hard fares the land to hastening ills a prey,
Where wealth accumulates, and men decay;
Princes and lords may flourish or may fade,
A breath can make them, as a breath has made;
But a bold peasantry their country's pride,
When once destroyed, can never be supplied."

On Goldsmith's poetry the judgment of the literary and the laity seem unanimous; both equally approve, and this is a rare consent. "The Traveller" and "The Deserted Village" are perfect in their kind; and of his shorter productions, "The Hermit" is a masterpiece of tenderness, and "Retaliation" a masterpiece of sagacity.

Goldsmith as a novelist has based an undying reputation upon one brief tale. Nor is this tale, critically considered, without grave defects. Parts of the plot are improbable; some of the incidents are even out of possibility, and much in each of the characters is inconsistent. "We cannot, for instance, conceive," Sir Walter Scott remarks, "how Sir William Thornhill should contrive to masquerade under the name of Burchill among his own tenantry, and upon his own estate; and it is absolutely impossible, to see how his nephew, the son, doubtless, of a younger brother (since Sir William inherited both title and property) should be nearly as old as the baronet himself. It may be added, that the character of Burchell, or Sir William Thornhill, is in itself extravagantly unnatural. A man of his benevolence would never have so long left his nephew in the possession of wealth, which he employed in the worst of purposes. Far less would he have permitted his scheme upon Olivia in a great measure to succeed, and that upon Sophia, also, to approach consummation; for, in the first instance, he does not interfere at all, and in the second his intervention is accidental."

This was a criticism from the highest of novelists, upon one who was the kindest. It is not, however, a criticism advanced with the technicalities of art; it is one which simple nature indicates, and which, if simple readers could not readily discover, they will readily admit. In what then consists the charm, which striking blemishes are not able to dissolve? It consists in that most beautiful creation of English fiction, "The Primrose Family." In this fascinating group, there is a spell which rivets our attention, and fixes our affections, and we cannot throw it off. We are bound to the Primroses and their originality of innocence, by the purity of their domestic life, and by the strength of their domestic love. Each of the Primroses is a decided and distinct individual. The Vicar has become known to us as a daily neighbor; the good Vicar, at once so heroic and so childlike; so simple, and yet so wise; so strong in the energy of the true, so gentle in the meekness of the holy. Beside him, in evil times and good, we have his loyal dame, who thought people ought to hold up their heads; whose cunning plots were open to all eyes but her own; who was proud of her sagacity, proud of her station, proud of her children, but prouder than all of her husband. Then we have George, the sage-errant of the family. We have the girls, "a glory and a joy" within their home, each different in her loveliness; Olivia, with such gladness in her laughter; Sophia, with such sweetness in her smiles. Moses, too, is a leading personage; Moses, half philosopher, and half a fool, who, like his father, could talk of the ancients, and like his mother "knew what he was about." Even little Dick and Bill, the privileged prattlers of the circle, have their places in the story, and the story needs them. And did ever another story, in such compass, touch so many emotions, and touch them so deeply? We laugh at its breadth of humor, we repose over its quiet pictures, and in a moment we are startled into weeping by its pathos. When the Vicar discovers the absence of his Olivia, his beautiful child, and his beloved, the spotless dove that but lately nestled in his bosom, who is not stunned at his madness, and exalted as he passes from madness to submission? When, from this, we trace him through the fire that leaves him houseless, to the prison where his eldest son lies chained for death; where his family gather about him in mourning and in want; how sublime, in every position, is his conduct, and how cheering are his words! With what heavenly mercy does he seek his fallen daughter; with what fatherly pity does he receive and shield her!

Not tired in alleviating the affliction which has bruised the hopes of his own house, he bears consolation to the wicked, with whom his own blameless lot is cast; he finds a brother in the assassin's cell, and in the felon's chains; for he finds in each a human being, and he wins him to repentance by the eloquence which evangelical sympathy alone inspires, and which evangelical sympathy alone can speak. His family companions, in his adversity, are transformed to his moral grandeur; his wife, chastened by suffering, lays aside her trifling, and shows herself a true-hearted woman. Even the rustic Moses, by his patient toil, not only earns the means of support for his imprisoned father, but for himself the meed of imperishable regard.

The humor of this tale is as delightful to cheer, as its wisdom is to instruct us. Nor does the wisdom lose force, but gains it in the humor by which it is relieved. The good Dr. Primrose seems himself aware, that people must smile at his zeal for "monogamy." Whiston had engraven on his wife's tomb, "that she was the only wife of William Whiston." "I wrote," says the Vicar, "a similar epitaph for my wife, though still living, in which I extolled her prudence, economy, and obedience, until death, and having got it copied fair, with an elegant frame, it was placed over the chimney-piece, where it answered several useful purposes. . . . It inspired her with a passion for fame, and constantly put her in mind of her end." Cousins to the fortieth degree claimed kindred, and had their claim allowed. Poor guests, well treated, make a happy company, and Dr. Primrose, was, " by nature, an admirer of happy faces. When the guest was not desirable a second time, the doctor says that he ever took care to lend him a riding coat, or a pair of boots, or sometimes a horse of small value ; " and I always," observes the good Vicar, " had the satisfaction of finding that he never came back to return them." Travellers, too, would sometimes step in to taste Mrs. Primrose's gooseberry wine ; " and I profess," says the Doctor, " on the veracity of a historian, that I never knew one of them find fault with it." The Doctor was as proud of his theory, as his spouse was of her gooseberry wine, and so lost a horse by his philosophical vanity.

" Are you, sir," inquired Jenkins, " related to the great Dr. Primrose, that courageous monogamist, the bulwark of the church ? "

" You behold, sir, before you, that Dr. Primrose, whom you are pleased to call great ; you see here that unfortunate divine, who has so long, and it would ill become me to say, so successfully, struggled against the deuterogamy of the age."

" Thou glorious pillar of unshaken orthodoxy ! " exclaims Jenkins ! "

Jenkins accepts the offer of his friendship ; with his friendship he takes his horse, in return giving him a false note for payment. The wisdom of the Vicar was a notable climax to the sagacity of the son; and an empty check on farmer Flamborough, was an appropriate counterpart from the same hand which had furnished the gross of green spectacles. Moses was the oracle of his mother. Moses, she said, always knew what he was about. How proudly he travelled up to the door, after his horse-dealing speculation, with his deal box upon his shoulder; with what quietude of success he received the salutations of his father.

"Well, Moses, my boy, what have you brought us from the fair?"

"Myself," cries Moses, with a sly look.

"Ah, Moses," cried my wife, "that we know, but where is the horse?"

"I have sold him," cried Moses, "for three pounds, five shillings, and two pence."

"Well done, my good boy," returned she, "I knew you would touch them off. Between ourselves, three pounds, five shillings, and two pence, is no bad day's work. Come, let us have it, then."

"I have brought back no money," cried Moses, again; "I have laid it all out in a bargain, and here it is," pulling out a bundle from his breast; "here they are, a gross of green spectacles, with silver rims and shagreen cases."

George was a worthy member of the same family, who went to Holland to teach English, and did not reflect until he landed, that it was necessary to know Dutch. And quite in keeping with all, was the family picture, which was first ordered to be of a certain size, and was then found to be too large for the house. The Flamboroughs were drawn, seven of them with seven oranges, "a thing quite out of taste, no variety in life, no composition in the world." We desired, says the Vicar, something in a brighter style, and then comes the detail.

"My wife," the Doctor observes, "desired to be represented as Venus, and the painter was desired not to be too frugal of his diamonds in her stomacher and hair. Her two little ones were to be Cupids by her side; while I, in my gown and bands, was to present her with my book on the Whistonian Controversy. Olivia would be drawn as an Amazon sitting on a bank of flowers, dressed in a green joseph, richly laced with gold, and a whip in her hand. Sophia was to be a shepherdess, with as many sheep as the painter would put in for nothing; and Moses was to be dressed out with a hat and white feather. Our taste so pleased the squire, that he insisted on being put in as one of the family, in the character of Alexander the Great, at Olivia's feet."

The character of Goldsmith is not of the most exalted kind, and though it is endeared to us from its simplicity, it does not command our highest admiration. It wanted self-denial; it therefore wanted the regulated foresight, the austere economy, by which lofty qualities are sustained and exercised. In virtues of the severe cast, that sacrifice is not the least, which, for the good of mankind, makes resignation of popular affections; and if we could perceive what great hearts have in this way endured, instead of esteeming them stoics, we would revere them as martyrs.

Goldsmith is one of those whom we cannot help liking, and whom we cannot criticize; yet he is one that should be praised with caution, if in our age there was much danger of his being imitated. We are too busy for meditative vagrancy; we are too practical for the delusions of scholarship; even with the felicitous genius of Goldsmith, the literary profession would now be an insecure basis for subsistence, and none at all for prodigality. Extent of competition, the rigor of criticism, the difficulty of acting on an immensely multiplied reading public, repress the efforts of vanity; yet, except in few instances, they do not compensate the efforts of power; the vain are driven to obscurity, but the powerful have little more than their fame. And though we possessed the abilities of Goldsmith, and were tempted to his follies, his life is before us for a memento, and his experience is sufficient for a warning. Yet is it agreeable to lay aside our prudence for a little, and enjoy with him, in fancy at least, the advantage of the hour; to participate in his thoughtless good nature, and to enter into his careless gayety; to sit with him in some lonely Swiss glen; or to listen to his flute among the peasantry of France; or to hear him debate logical puzzles in monastic Latin; to share the pride of his new purple coat, which Johnson would not praise, and which Boswell could not admire. More grateful still, is the relief which we derive from the perusal of his works; for in these we have the beauty of his mind, and no shade upon its wisdom; the sweetness of humanity, and its dignity also.

We need the mental refreshment, which writers like Goldsmith afford. Our active and our thoughtful powers are all on the stretch; and such, unless it has appropriate relaxations, is not a state of nature or a state of health. From the troubles of business, which absorb the attention or exhaust it; from the acclivities of society, which exemplify, in the same degrees, the force of mechanism and the force of will; from the clamor of politics, from the asperity of religious discussions, we turn to philosophy and literature for less fatiguing or less disquieting interests. But our philosophy, when not dealing with matter, is one which, in seeking the limits of reason, carries it ever into the infinite and obscure ; our literature is one which, in its genuine forms, has equal intensity of passion and intensity of expression ; which, in its spurious forms, mistakes extravagance for the one, and bombast for the other. Our genuine literature is the production of natural causes, and has its peculiar excellence. But from the excitement of our present literature, whether genuine or spurious, it is a pleasant change to take up the tranquil pages of Goldsmith ; to feel the sunny glow of his thoughts upon our hearts, and on our fancies the gentle music of his words. In laying down his writings, we are tempted to exclaim, "O that the author of 'The Deserted Village' had written more poetry ! O that the author of 'The Vicar of Wakefield' had written more novels ! "

SPIRIT OF IRISH HISTORY.*

It is now some years since I began to speak in Boston. Among the first of my efforts, Ireland was my theme. I endeavored, as best I could, to tell her story. I was heard with generous interest, but it was the story, and not the teller, that inspired it. It was called for throughout the length and breadth of New England; it was repeated in city halls and in village lyceums. Old and young, grave and gay, listened to it with open ears and with eager hearts; and to many of them it seemed a new and wild and strange recital. It is no longer novel. It is now, not a story, but a drama; a black and fearful drama, which civilized nations gaze upon with a terrified astonishment, that has no power to weep. It was then gloomy and sad enough, and to those who know life only in its general comforts, it appeared a condition which it would be hard to render worse. But the presumptuousness of man is con-

* This Lecture was given for relief of the Irish poor, in 1847.

stantly rebuked by the vicissitude of events. It is but too surely so in this case. There was yet the vial of a deeper woe in store, and that vial is now open. Tragic as the story of Ireland was, when first I tried to tell it, it might yet be given with those flashes of mirth and wit, those outburstings of fun, and drollery, and oddity, and humor, which can be crushed in the Irish heart only by the heaviest load of sorrow. Of such weight is now the burden that lies upon it.

Ireland, now, is not simply a place of struggle, of want, of hard work, and of scanty fare, it has become a wilderness of starvation. The dreariest visitation which humanity can receive, rests upon it — not of fire, not of the sword, not of the plague; but that, compared with which, fire, and sword, and plague, are but afflictions; that is, Hunger — hunger, that fell and dreadful thing, which, in its extremity, preys more horribly on the mind, even than the body; which causes friend to look on friend with an evil eye, and the heart of a maiden to be stern to her lover; and the husband to glare upon the wife that nestled in his bosom, and the mother to forget her sucking child. Such, though we trust never to come to this awful extremity, is the nature of that calamity, which lately has been preying upon Ireland. It has not indeed come to this awful extremity, but it has approached far enough towards it, to spread over that beautiful island a pall of mourning; far enough towards it, to quench the joy of childhood, to bow down the strength of men, to wither the loveliness of women, to take away the comeliness of the young, and to cover the heads of the aged with a sorrow darker than the grave. We cannot think of it with other thoughts than those of grief. We cannot refer to it with other speech than that of sadness. For my own part, I cannot hear of this terrible affliction; I cannot read of it; my imagination, of its own accord, transports me into the midst of it, and, for the time, I dwell in the company and throngs of the wretched. The necessity that compels me to think and speak of it, bows down my soul to the earth, and I am almost prompted to exclaim, in the words of the prophet, "O, that my head were waters, and my eyes were fountains of tears, that I might weep day and night for the slain of the daughters of my people."

Multitudes are perishing; that fact admits neither of doubt nor of dispute. Multitudes are perishing; that fact is as certain as it is terrible. It does not signify what they are or where, the fact is still most horrible and most appalling. Were they savages in the depths of an African wilderness, our common humanity would urge us to send them succor. Were they the most utter strangers, foreign to us in every mode of thought and habit, that can render nations alien to each other, they would still be within the embrace of that common humanity, and its voice would plead for them. Were they most base and worthless, both in character and condition, their misfortunes would give them dignity, and win from us compassion. Were they enemies, and had done us the worst of injuries, not only the precepts of the Gospel, but the sentiments of magnanimity, would impel us to help them in the hour of their agony. But they are none of these. They have given to civilization some of its most quickening elements; some of its most brilliant genius; some of its fairest ornaments; some of its most heroic minds. Numbers of us, here, are bone of their bone, and flesh of their flesh; the fathers who supported our youth, live above, or lie below, the green sward of Erin; the mothers who sang our infancy to sleep with its plaintive melodies, are still breathing its air, or gone to mingle with its saints in heaven. To all of us, of whatever nation, they are kindred in the ties of that solemn existence, which we feel the more intensely, the more it is afflicted. They are a people, too, whose own ears have been always open to the cry of the distressed. They have ever been willing to give, not merely of their abundance, but even of their want; a people whose hospitality is free as the wind upon their mountains, and generous as the rain upon their valleys; the fame of it as wide as the earth, and as old as their history. This people are now in grievous troubles. They are in the midst of famine, and we are in the midst of plenty. Out of this great plenty we are sending them support, and with support our pity and our prayers. Let us most gratefully and humbly bless God, who has put this most blessed privilege in our power; the privilege of saving those who are ready to perish, and of causing thousands of breaking hearts to sing for joy; to change mourning to gladness, and the spirit of heaviness for the spirit of praise.

I am not here to excite an interest; for that is already excited, and has been working bravely through the land with a passionate emotion. It has been shaking the hearts of this great people to the utmost verge of their dominion; agitating, not their cities alone, but piercing the sympathies of those who dwell in shanties on the open prairie, and by the half cleared forest; melting into tenderness, not the women of the land alone, but subduing the hardy men of the woods, of the camp, of the ship, and of the battle-field. I would not insult your sympathies by appealing to them; I would not insult your generosity by praising it; I am not here to plead a cause. Humanity in millions of hearts have effectually pleaded that cause already; and hands are lifted up, while now I speak, to thank Heaven, and the good humanity in which Heaven lives on earth, for the sympathy with which it has responded to the cries of afflicted brotherhood.

I will not therefore enlarge on the present distress; I will not, and I cannot, go into its technical detail; neither will I vaguely ascribe this great suffering to Providence. I will not seek the sources of it in the clouds above, or in the earth beneath; I will try, so far as my light leads me, to seek those sources in directions where they may be intelligibly accounted for. I would lay no blame on the present generation; I do not speak of them. I am not insensible to the great exertions of the Government of the British nation to meet the tremendous crisis now existing; nor would I speak otherwise than in heartfelt, enthusiastic sympathy of those huge manifestations of kindness in the British nation, which show forth those sublime charities, that vindicate the divine and God-imaged character of our nature. I will endeavor to review the whole system, of which the present distress is a part, and of which it is a result; I will endeavor to seek out whence it has originated, and how it may be changed; I will endeavor to trace some of its causes, and to indicate some of its remedies. I must, of course, confine myself to a few striking points, not alone by the limits of our time, but by the requirements of the occasion. The occasion is one, that will not tolerate much that admits greatly of dispute; it is one that requires all the conciliation which truth can sanction. It will therefore be my desire, in analyzing causes, and in specifying remedies, to take as broad and common ground as, with my opinions, it is possible for me to take. It will be also my desire to give no candid or just man offence; and though such a man may dispute my positions, I trust that he will have no complaint to make against my spirit, or against my temper.

The causes of Irish distress many find wholly in the character of the people. On this topic, we cannot afford to enlarge; and that it may not stand in our way as we proceed, we will grant, for the sake of argument, that the character of the people is as idle and as reckless as these philosophers describe it, and still it will be seen that, to ascribe the state of Ireland to this cause alone, or to this cause mainly, is not only partial but false; at variance alike with any comprehensive grasp of sound logic or personal observation. The cause of any particular suffering in Ireland is seldom local or temporary, seldom to be found within itself or near it. The causes even of the present destitution are not all immediate; they are not all in the failure of the potato crop, not all in the character of those who plant the potato and live on it. The potato, it is true, is a precarious vegetable, and the people of Ireland, who have fed upon it for generations, are not in all things the wisest and most provident of nations; but in any sound state of things, it would not, surely, be within the limits of any contingency, that millions should wither into the dust, which had failed to afford nourishment to a fragile root. Such afflictions as Ireland is now enduring, terrible as they are, are not singular in her experience. They have been but too often her misfortune; and though, to our view, they are strange, they are, in her story, sufficiently familiar. But these afflictions come not from the skies above or the earth beneath; and, therefore, we shall not ascend to the heavens, nor go down to the deep, to seek their causes. Most of them are within the range of very ordinary inquiry, and they are both intelligible and explainable. I shall speak on causes of two kinds; one historical, and one social.

And, first, of the historical. Ireland has long been a country of agitation. The elements of discord were sown early in her history; and throughout her course, they have been nourished, and not eradicated. At first, divided into small principalities, like all countries so circumstanced, strife was constantly taking place among them, either for dominion or defence. It did not happen to Ireland as to England, that these separate states had been subdued into unity by a native prince, before the intrusion of a foreign ruler. It did not happen to Ireland as to England, that the foreign ruler took up his residence in it, identified his dignity with it, and that his children became natives of the soil. England, previous to the invasion of William the Conqueror, was a united empire, and therefore, though at the battle of Hastings, the occupant of the throne was changed, the integrity of the nation remained. Ireland was made up of divided and conflicting states, when the myrmidons of Henry the Second arrived upon its shores ; and, even after these had gained settlements in the country, there was no adhesive principle among the natives. Had Ireland been consolidated, she could not have been conquered ; or, being conquered, she would, like England, have absorbed the conquerors. The spirit of English nationality was never stronger than it was in the princes of the Norman line ; and they asserted it with a haughtiness, oftentimes with an injustice, that rendered them formidable to every neighboring state. They were the most inordinately jealous of any interference with the concern of their kingdom, either of a secular or a spiritual character ; for generations they guarded England with even a ferocious pride, but, also, with a commendable zeal, they reared up her native institutions, and brought out her latent energies.

But the stranger came to Ireland, and a stranger he still remained. English dominion commenced in Ireland in a spirit of conquest, and it continued in a spirit of exclusion. National animosity thus perpetuated, sustained the spirit of war, and war raged on with a fierceness which time did nothing to mitigate. The native chieftains, when not in conflict among themselves, united against the common foe ; and the end of every new struggle was increased oppression to the people. Covetousness was added to the other baser passions ; and rapacity inflamed the anarchy in which it hoped for gain. Defeated rebellion brought confiscation ; insurrection was, therefore, the harvest of adventurers ; soldiers of fortune, or rather soldiers for fortune, gathered like wolves to the battle. They were ready to glory in the strife and to profit by it ; they enjoyed the soil of the wretches whom they slaughtered, and the work seemed as great a pleasure as the recompense. Exhausted, however, in robbing the aborigines, they sought new excitement in despoillng one another ; and, tired of fighting for plunder, they began at last to fight for precedence. So it continued to the period of Elizabeth, and though that brought change, it did not bring improvement ; for to the conflict of race was now added the conflict of religion.

This age of Elizabeth, which was to Europe the dawn of many hopes — this age of Elizabeth, which was so adorned and so enriched with all that makes an age transcendent — this age of Elizabeth was only for Ireland a heavy and a starless night. The government of Elizabeth, which had so much glory for England, gave no promise to Ireland. Under the sway of Elizabeth, Ireland lay in tempest and in waste. Oppression, that makes wise men mad, will provoke even despair to resistance, and resistance was obstinate and frequent in Ireland to the rulers whom Elizabeth set above them. Resistance was put down by methods the most inhuman; the crops were destroyed, dwelling-houses burned, the population indiscriminately massacred, famine the most terrible ensued, and hunger withered those whom the sword had spared. The people were slaughtered, but not subdued; the soil was not enriched, but ravaged; no arts arose; no principles of wealth or liberty were developed; life was unsafe; and property in the true sense was scarcely known. Even the stony heart of Elizabeth at length was touched; humanity, for once, shot a pang to her breast. "Alas, alas!" she cried; "I fear lest it be objected to us, as it was to Tiberius, concerning the Dalmatian commotions

— you, you, it is who are to blame, who have committed your flock, not to shepherds, but to wolves." And to wolves, they were still committed. Such was the rigor of the ordinary government, that a deputy of the most common kindness, gained the worship of the unhappy Irish, and became hateful to the jealous queen; so that the gratitude of the people ruined, at the same time, their benefactors and themselves. And yet, this age of Elizabeth was a glorious age. Everywhere, but in Ireland, it was filled with power and with promise. From the death of Mary to that of James the First, was a period such as comes but seldom, and when it comes such as makes an era. A mighty life was palpitating among the nations; the head of civilized humanity was filled with many speculations, and the heart was beating with marvellous fancies and magnanimous passions. Genius and glory had burst as a flood of light upon the world. The feudal system was passing away. The arm of its oppression had been broken, but its high-bred courtesy yet remained; its violence was repressed, but its heroic spirit had not been quenched. The courage of the savage warrior had given way before the chivalry of the humaner soldier. The dominion of superstition, too, had been broken, but a rigid utilitarianism had not yet taken place. The spectres of night had vanished, but dreams of the wonderful and the lovely still hovered around imagination. The earth was not bare, nor the heavens empty. The merchant and the money-changer began to rule the city; but Queen Mab was not yet dethroned. She had yet her fairy empire in the green-wood shade; she had yet her dancing in the moonlit glen. The practical had not yet banished the romantic, and the soul had her philosophy, as well as the senses. Columbus had opened new worlds, and the old world hailed him as the Moses of the seas. Dreams of sunny regions; of Edens in the desert; of El Doradoes in the treadless hills, wafted longing fancies from olden homes, and thoughts flew fast and far on the crest of the wave and the wings of the wind. Learning started from leaden sleep to earnest life. Philosophy poured forth her eloquent wisdom; and the thoughtful listened with enraptured ear. Poetry was filling the earth with her music; and Fiction was delighting mankind with rare enchantment; and Religion was busying all brains with her solemn and profound discoursing. Bacon was sounding the depths of human intellect, and calling from their silence the energies of endless progression. Shakspeare was shaping, to enduring beauty, those wondrous creations which embody the universal life of man. Cervantes, the glorious Spaniard, in soul a brother to the glorious Briton, had sent forth among men's fancies, Don Quixote and Sancho Panza ; the high-dreaming knight, and the low-thinking squire ; the grave in company with the grotesque, a goodly image of humanity for everlasting laughter and everlasting love. Luther had arisen, awful and gigantic, half the earth his platform, and millions of excited men his audience. Liberty had begun to know her rights, and was gathering courage to maintain them. Traditional claims had already lost in the contest against natural justice. Priests and princes had ceased to be gods, and the people were fast rising to be men. Commerce had enlarged her boundaries ; wealth had increased its enterprise ; independence had grown with industry. The course of freedom went nobly onward. Britain had humbled Spain ; and Holland, after one of the most heroic struggles in the history of patriotism, had cast off the Spanish yoke. While Europe was thus rejoicing in spreading grandeur, the fairest island on its western border, with every means of prosperity and glory, lay like a ruin at moonlight, where pirates had assembled to divide their plunder in blasphemy and in blood.

James of Scotland, the successor of his mother's slayer, treated unfortunate Ireland with no gentler policy. Without accusation of sedition or rebellion, he alienated six counties from their owners, and colonized them with his countrymen. The outcasts wandered on their own soil, as strangers and as vagabonds. Fearful deeds were done in revenge and retribution during the terrible insurrection of 1641, which occurred in the reign of this man's son. Deadly passions mingled together in the strife, as elements in the hurricane ; and the blood of reformer and the blood of Romanist, swelled the common torrent. England, too, became convulsed with trouble. Charles endeavored to ingratiate the Irish, and to a considerable extent he succeeded. But, their assistance availed the unhappy monarch nothing ; and ere his blood was wellnigh clotted on the block, they had Cromwell of the iron hand, dealing death upon themselves.

It is not my province, here, even if my power answered to the task, to draw a complete moral portrait of Cromwell. I am simply to speak of him in relation to Ireland ; and, in that relation, he was a steel-hearted exterminator. I have no inclination to deny him grandeur, and if I had, the general verdict would stand independently of my inclination. Whether the moralist approve, or whether he condemn, the world always enthrones will and power and success ; and that which it enthrones, it worships. How much in Cromwell was the honesty of a patriot, how much was the policy of a designer ; how much was purity, how much was ambition, which so predominated, the evil or the good, as to constitute his character; this will probably be decided in opposite directions by opposite parties to the end of history. Whatever be the decision on the man, measured as a whole, the facts of his career in Ireland show him to have been most cruel and most sanguinary.

Nor are these facts inconsistent with our general idea of the dictator's character. A dark compound of the daring soldier and the religious zealot, uniting in one spirit the austerest attributes of each, stern in purpose, and rapid in execution, he was the man for a mission of destruction. The Irish, on many accounts, were peculiarly hateful to him. They were the adherents of defeated royalty. They were not simply prelatists, which were in itself offensive; but they were papists, and that was hideous iniquity. They were not only aliens, they were worse than aliens; they were outcasts, the doomed of prophecy, the sealed of Antichrist. They were the modern Canaanites, and he was the modern Joshua, the anointed of the Lord, to deal judgment on the reprobate; and judgment he dealt with vengeance, with vengeance that knew no touch of mercy. His track in Ireland may be followed over ruins which yet seem fresh. We can trace him as we do a ravenous animal, by the blotches where he lay to rest, or by the bloody fragments where he tore his prey. The Irish peasantry still speak of this man with those vivid impressions, which, of all passions, terror alone can leave. They allude to him in the living phraseology, which only that can prompt which moves us nearly, and, therefore, moves us strongly; they allude to him, not as if he were a shadow in the dimness of two centuries, but as if he were an agent of recent days. Stop, as you pass a laborer on the road-side in Ireland; ask him to tell you of the ruin before you on the hill. You will hear him describe it in language far more poetical and far more picturesque than I can copy, but somewhat in manner such as this: "Och, sure, that 's the castle o' the Cogans, that Cromwell, the blackguard, took away from them. But maybe they did 'nt fight, while fightin' was in them, the poor fellows; barrin' there 's no strivin' agin the devil, the Lord presarve us, and everybody knows that Cromwell, bad win to him, was hand and glove wid the ould boy; musha, faix, he was, as sure as there 's fish in the say, or pigs in Connaught. There 's the hill where the wagabond planted his cannon. There 's the farm which the Blaneys got for sellin' the Pass, the white-livered thraitors; there 's the brache which he made in the walls, where brave Square Cogan — a bed in heaven to his soul — was killed, wid his six fine darlant sons, as strappin' boys as you 'd meet in a long summer's day. Och, wirra, wirra, struh; bud Cogan was a man it would do your heart good to see; my vardi av, it would n't keep the frosht out of your stomach the blackest day in winther; full and plinty were in his house, and the poor never went impty from his door; as I heard my grandmother say, that heard it from her grandmother, that, be the same token, was Cogan's cousin. Och, bud, with fair fighting, Cogan did n't fear the face of .man, and, sure enough, when Cromwell commanded him to surrender, he tould infarnal coppernose, he 'd ate his boots first; throth he would, and his stockings after, av there was the laste use in it; bud the man 's not born'd of woman, that can stand against a whelp of hell; and, av ould Nick iver had a son, my word for it bud his name was Oliver."

The cause of the Stuarts, that family so faithless to their friends, and so fatal to themselves, next made Ireland the battle-ground of faction. Again her green hills were sown with blood; again her pleasant valleys were scorched with famine. The infatuated Catholics joined that wretched imbecile, James the Second, while the Protestants, with a wiser policy, gathered to the standard of William the Dutchman, the son-in-law of James, and his opponent. The fortunes of James received their first blow at the siege of Derry in the north; were staggered at the battle of the Boyne, midway in the kingdom; and were fatally decided at the taking of Limerick in the south. The fall of Limerick closed the war. James had fled; and William remained the victor. Limerick did not go out of the contest ignominiously. Even the women threw themselves into the breach, and for that time saved the city; nor did the city, itself, surrender, but on terms which comprehended the whole of Ireland. Limerick capitulated on the part of all the Irish Catholics. The capitulation was but signed, when a large French fleet appeared in the river, with extensive supplies and numerous reinforcements. But with the good faith of honorable men, fifteen thousand laid down their arms, and were true to their engagements. The terms of this treaty were fair and advantageous. They secured to the Catholics the rights of property, of liberty, and of conscience, and all things seemed to augur well for peace, for unity, and for happiness.

Had the victors been merciful with power, and generous with success, had they been just, nay, had they been wisely politic, Ireland might have been tranquillized, and her prosperity might have commenced. But it was an age of faction, and faction was true to its vilest instincts. The legislation that followed this event, was intensely exclusive, and it was exclusively Protestant. The whole power of the country was in the hands of a Protestant aristocracy. The first action, then, of the Parliament in Ireland, after the reduction of Limerick, was to annul the treaty of Limerick, a treaty as solemn as any that history records ; a treaty made in the face of armies, and which pledged the faith of nations. And, not only that, but it was followed by a code of laws, which would have been a shame upon the reign of Nero ; a code of laws which made, at one time, the Catholic religion a capital offence ; and which, when greatly mitigated, denied to Catholics the means of education, the claims of property, and the rights of citizens. Legislation like this was, of course, disastrous. Strange, indeed, if it were not. If it were not, history were a lie, and all experience a dream ; if it were not, human nature were, itself, a confounding delusion. It was disastrous to the Protestant religion, which it pretended to support ; it was disastrous to the interests of England, which it promised to maintain ; it was disastrous, also, to the unhappy people whose energies it crushed ; but, that the law of compensation should not utterly fail — that some evidence should be given to earth, that even on earth crime does not go unpunished — it was disastrous to its enactors.

Man can never separate himself from his fellows. He can never make their evil his good. The darkness which he draws upon his country, will overshadow his own home ; and the misery which he prepares for his neighbor, will be misery for himself. So it was with the authors of these evil laws; so it ever must be, while moral right binds actions to appropriate consequences, while a God of eternal justice governs the world by principles which are as immutable as they are holy. The possessions which rapine had acquired, and which wrong controlled, did not give such return as the covetous heart desired. By confiscation, by penalties, by all modes of harsh restriction, the kingdom was drained of its native intelligence and native strength. Wealth of sentiment, wealth of capital, wealth of skill, wealth of industry, wealth of muscle, were driven from the country, or paralyzed within it. The high chivalry which generous treatment would have retained, directed foreign courts, commanded foreign armies; while a hardy yeomanry that indulgence could have made loyal forever, carried bravery to the ranks of England's enemies, and labor to their markets.

And, observe with what a solemn retribution the consequences return upon the class who enacted or favored this kind of legislation. The laws against Catholics pressed upon the whole tenantry of Ireland, for the whole tenantry of Ireland were, and are Catholic. The laws, therefore, against the Catholics, were so many enactments against the interests of the landlords themselves ; were, in fact, so many tariffs against their wealth. Uncertainty of title disturbed industry; the soil withered under imperfect cultivation; absentee-ism of proprietors left the laborers without protection, and the owners without profit. Only meagre harvests were gathered from exhausted fields. Trade had no scope in impoverished cities; the peasantry were starving, and the gentry were poor. This gentry, poor, but luxurious, lived upon estates that were miserably deteriorated, as if they were in pristine freshness; and doing nothing to enrich the soil, they would have from it the utmost rents; and thence they became indebted, and thence they became embarrassed. To dig they were not able, but to beg they were not ashamed. They begged pensions, places, sinecures; and no work was so unjust or mean, which they were not willing to do for government, if government was liberal enough in patronage. Gaming, gormandizing, profanity, licentiousness, became aristocratic distinctions. Honor there was to kill, but not honesty to pay; and the man who shot his friend for an inadvertent word, could bear, if any thing was to be gained by it, the reiterated insolence of a viceroy's menial. The wages being ready, here was the hireling; and the slave, in his turn, became the tyrant. The self-respect which he lost as a time-server, he sought, after the manner of all low natures, to regain as an oppressor; and the hardship of the forlorn serf paid for the mortification of the suppliant official. These men who, in element and charitable duties, might have been as gods, enjoying and dispensing blessings, taking the evil way of persecution, found their due reward in being despised by those whom they served, and in being detested by those whom they governed.

If any one shall think this tone exaggerated, then I ask him to look at the Memoirs of Sir Jonah Barrington, in which he may study, at his leisure, the manners of the Irish gentlemen in the last century; the picture, too, is painted by one of themselves; by one who shared all their partialities for combat and for claret, for pensions and for place.

Events rapidly proceeded to bring relief to Ireland, and partially to bring freedom. Cornwallis was captured at Yorktown, and America sprung into her glory from a province to a nation. The volunteers arose in Ireland, and forty thousand, with arms in their hands, demanded independence. Henry Grattan gave their passions sublime expression. Corruption was startled from the apathy of indulgence, and the guilty were struck with fear as with the voice of a prophet. Grattan called Ireland up from the dust of most servile degradation. He put brave words into her mouth, and a new hope into her heart; and although upon his own lips the words afterwards sunk into complaint, and the hope withered to despondency, he was not the less heroic on that account. Speaking at one time of Ireland, he asserts that she is a nation. Speaking of her again, he says, "I sat by her cradle, I followed her hearse;" but always he was her champion, and he was her friend. Lowly as she was when he entered upon life, he determined that she should not so remain. He caused her to arise, august and majestic, before her tyrants, bound as she was with their sackcloth. He called on her to assume her might, and taught her the strength that yet slumbered in her breast. He was the fearless accuser of her enemies. He dragged the villains into open light, that trampled on her rights, and that battened on her miseries. He loved her with an enthusiasm that only death could quench. She was the passion of his soul, the devotion of his life. Mighty in his eloquence, he was yet mightier in his patriotism.

The effects of his eloquence are left in the history of his country; and in me it would be vain, as it would be impertinent, to describe, in my feeble words, the power of such speech as his — speech that made the proudest quail — speech that shivered and prostrated the most able and the most iniquitous faction, which personal selfishness and political corruption ever banded together in gainful wickedness. Rapid, intense, scornful, indignant, his spirit was formed for contest. Fiery in passion, and brilliant in intellect, his antithetic language shot forth as lightning, as beautiful and as fatal. Of stern and stoic grandeur, he was the reformer who was wanted among evil, exalted, and educated men. He was not of the gladsome fancy, which gathers flowers and weaves a garland; he was of the impetuous temper which rises upon the storm, and plays among the clouds. With individuals, he may not always have been in the right, and with his country he was never in the wrong.

The French Revolution came, then, to rock political Europe with its tremendous earthquake. Hoary dynasties rocked on their foundations. Decrepid legitimacy trembled and looked aghast. The terrible insurrection of 1798 brought fresh desolation to Ireland. Some interludes of jail and gibbet being gone through, an afterpiece was added to this horrible drama in 1830, signalized by the death of Lord Kilwarden, and by the execution of the noble-hearted Emmett. You all know the story of his heroism and his love; you know how he fell in the prime of a most manly nature; you know how a true and beautiful spirit laid her broken heart upon his grave. Your own Washington Irving has told you this in words of rainbow light; your own

Irving, whose liberal genius loves the good of every land; and when he gives their annals, none can add beauty to the record. You have the ashes of an exiled Emmett among you; shrouded on the soil of liberty, he lies in sacred sleep. You gave him in life a freeman's home; in death you have given him a patriot's grave.

Among the mighty spirits which have been lights to Ireland, I will mention one who, in this sad period, was preëminent. I allude to Curran, the glory of the Irish bar. Most exalted in his oratory, and most generous in his use of it, he was ever what the true man would wish to be — if his power enabled him, the defender of liberty, the champion of the wronged. With a moral intellect of the widest grasp, he had an imagination of subtle delicacy and of gorgeous wealth; and this intellect, impulsive with a superhuman fervor, and this imagination, lyrical as the very soul of poetry, became, in their union, an enthusiasm that dared the loftiest heights and gained them. But, though soaring, it was not solitary. If it mounted upwards to the skies, it was borne thither on the aspirations of all generous interests. It carried others to its own proud climbings; and they, for the moment, transported from the lower earth, burned with its electric fire, and became godlike in its communicated lustre. How various is the eloquence in which that opulent spirit found expression. It is wit, ready and exhaustless; piercing as the pointed steel, or lambent as a ray of light; now playful as a gleeful child, and then mischievous as a merry fiend. It is humor, in all queer analogies, in all shapes of oddity, in all lights and hues of fantasy. It is sarcasm, which lashes its victim to despair. It is pathos, which wrings the heart; which touches it in every nerve, where agony is borne; which searches it in every fold where the smallest drop of grief can lie concealed. It is denunciation. And, here he is greatest of all. How does he exhibit the wrong-doer! How does he show the transgressor his ways! How does he display the tortures of an accusing conscience, the sickness of a guilty soul, the apathy of habit, the damnation of remorse!

And no matter who the wrong-doer is, let him tremble, if Curran is to paint his deeds. Proud he may be in titles, boundless in wealth, hardened in the bronze of fashion; if he is human, the orator's words shall transfix him; wherever feeling has a sense, a barb shall rankle; and for the time, at least, he shall stand before the world, naked, bleeding, shivering, and despised; to his species a thing of scorn, and to himself a thing of shame. Office shall no more protect him than rank. Is he a judge, who sullies the purity of the bench with the malice of a partisan? His ermine shall not guard him from the advocate's indignation; and the tribunal which he disgraces, shall in its very loftiness, but make his ignominy the more conspicuous. Neither shall a villain find a shield in the baseness of his work or the obscurity of his condition. Is he a spy, whom government pays for perjury, the hireling violator of human faith and human nature — a wretch that panders for the gallows, and steeps his feet in widows' and in orphans' tears? Cased and coated as his heart may be in adamant, callous as may be his brutish face, stolid as may be his demon-soul, Curran could cleave the armor of his wickedness, and shake his miscreant spirit with fear, when it had lost even the memory of a virtue.

It is not, however, the power of Curran's eloquence, but the purpose of it, which has relation to this lecture. It was for the weak against the strong. Curran lived in times which tried men's souls, and many souls there were, which did not stand the trial. Some, with coward fear, sank before the storm of power; and others, with selfish pliancy, dissolved in the sunshine of patronage. But Curran was brave as he was incorruptible. In 1798, he labored with a martyr's patience, and with a hero's courage. He pleaded under the shadow of the scaffold. He defended one client over the dead body of another; and while the victim is expiring on the gallows, for whom yesterday he struggled, with no hope to cheer his labor, he struggles as manfully to-day for one who will be the victim of to-morrow. He was upright, when honor was rebellion; he was true, when integrity was treason; he stood by the accused and the doomed, when to pity was to participate; and he was loyal to liberty, when even to name her, was almost to die.

The year 1829 saw the Catholic emancipated, and now he stands with other British subjects, in equality of privilege and equality of grievance. The later history of Ireland has had three grand epochs, and in each has had a man fashioned for the time. In 1781, the Parliament of Ireland contended for independence; then there arose the majestic spirit of immortal Grattan; all that was claimed, he asserted, and all that he asserted, he achieved. In 1798, the liberty of the citizens was set at nought; the impetuous voice of Curran arose above the storm, and if it was not able to quell injustice, it bore witness to the right. In 1829, six millions were emancipated, and, with that sublime event, the name of O'Connell is forever associated. But, not with that year or that event alone, the name of O'Connell is connected with the indefatigable struggle of half a century; it is not only sacred in the liberty of his country, but in the liberty of man; and the fame of it will become wider and brighter, as freedom covers the earth, and a slave is not known in the world.

The historical aspect of our subject, presents us with nothing but disunion and mismanagement; and the social, to which we must now briefly refer, presents us with nothing better. We observe, in the structure of Irish society, not merely that the elements of it are fragmentary, but antagonistic. There is, for instance, little of native aristocracy; and there is no country on the earth, which so respects and reverences its mighty names. The old families, Celtic and Saxon, were successively stripped of their estates. It was asserted by Chancellor Fitzgibbon, that the island had changed owners three times in a century. The aristocracy in Ireland, have, therefore, stood apart from the people. Their existence is entirely a separate one; their education is distinct; their feelings are anti-national; their sympathies are foreign; they are aliens after two centuries of possession. No people are more easily governed than the Irish through their imagination and affections. Appeal successfully to these faculties, and you may rule them as you please. If you would have power with the English, appeal to their interests; show to them that you can lessen their taxes, and that you can increase their loaf. If you would gain power with the Irish, appeal to their sentiments; show them that you would bring back to Ireland, the glory that has departed; that you would re-string their national Harp; and re-kindle her national oratory; that you would rebuild the Halls of Tara, and flood them with the music of her bards; that you would re-open the doors of her senate, and fill its courts with the eloquence of her statesmen.

But, to understand a people, you must live with them; nay, you must have within you the life of their life; and without this understanding of a people, you will vainly try to work on their sentiments. You can work on their sentiments only by sympathy. You must freely appreciate their virtues; you must have that also in you, which can penetrate the spirit even of their vices. Herein was the power of O'Connell. It was not all in the genius of the man; nor was it all in the wrongs of the government. Much of the secret lay in the profound insight which he ever had of the character of the people; the complete identification of his nature with theirs. His words were resistless, for they were the echoes of the hearts around him, and with the beatings of these hearts, his own heart kept time. The Irish aristocrat has no such unity with the people; nay, he has scarcely an external acquaintance with them. He has not the affection of a native, and he wants the impartiality of a stranger. His life is a sort of penance for his birth. He would not be an Irishman, and he cannot be an Englishman. He looks splenetically across the channel, and mourns that his trooper-ancestor gave him any thing in Ireland but its acres. He then turns a sullen gaze upon the soil on which he has had the misfortune to be born, and which has had the still greater misfortune to bear him. He is to his tenantry, not so much a protector as a superior; a claimant rather than a patron; an exactor more than an improver; always a receiver, and seldom a bestower.

This opposition of interior feeling between the higher and lower classes in Ireland, is lamentably exemplified by a corresponding contrast of external circumstances. Irish society is a living antithesis, of which the peer and the peasant are no fanciful extremes. The peasant shows what privations life can endure; the peer, with what indulgence it can become a burden. The peasant works, but does not eat; the peer eats, but does not work. The food of the peasant is, also, the food of the brutes; that of the peer were a banquet for the gods. The peasant sows, and reaps, and gathers into barns, and carries the crop to market, and carries nothing home; the peer sows not, reaps not, gathers not into barns, carries not the crop to market, and has all the gain without even the trouble of carrying it home. It makes some difference to the peer, whether his territory is fertile or barren; for he has whatever it produces; it makes none to the peasant, for small crop or abundant, his lot is still the same, to toil and to starve. The manor houses of the Irish gentry are situated in the midst of extensive domains, surrounded by lofty walls, and guarded by surly gate-keepers. The finest of these places are often girded by deserts of the most squalid misery. The owners are in them on rare occasions, and then, it is to revel in the midst of want.

Suppose yourself a guest on one of these occasions. Look around you on the scene! The princely park without, and the ornamented halls within; slope, woodland, garden, hill, dale, and river, glowing in the outward prospect; the inward view, that of a kingly residence furnished for every refined desire; adorned with mirrors, statues, pictures, replenished with whatever can delight the fancy or feast the senses. Think, then, of a tenant peasantry, physically more deplorable than the serfs of Turkey; and when you have thus thought, look calmly on the assembly before you. Here, gathered at joyous night, is a throng of the noble and the fair; men of gallant bearing, and women of surpassing beauty. Lights stream over decorations which almost transcend what eastern story feigned of eastern magic; music floats upon the perfumed air, and grace rules the mazes of the dance. When you recollect the haggard country through which you passed, to arrive at such a mansion; when you recollect the hovels that afflicted you on the way, the sad faces that stared you, as you went along, that constantly subdued your reveries to grief; when you recollect the fever and the hunger, that, as you travelled by then, appalled your very soul; all that you see in this abode of grandeur, appears unnatural; it seems a brilliant, and yet an agonizing vision; an illusion by some evil genius, powerful to delight, terrible to destroy. You cannot reconcile it with your ordinary associations — with your sentiments of moral harmony; it is incongruous; a rejoicing in an hospital, a feast in a famine-ship, a dance in a charnel-house, a bridal in a sepulchre; your heart becomes convulsed, your head giddy, your imagination confused and sick. You look upon a social class that bewilders you, and you turn from the whole with loathing and disgust.

The social system in Ireland is disjointed and defective. The great proprietors are absentees, and the small ones are impoverished. Another decisive evil in the social state of Ireland is, the want of due gradation. Where there is not general equality, there ought to be successive ranks. But society in Ireland exists only in extremes. The two main divisions of it are the owners of the soil, and its occupiers; and between these there seems a gulf, which one cannot pass to companion with the other. To fill up this wide interval, there is wanted an active and enterprising middle class. Except in the learned professions, social eminence in Ireland belongs only to the ownership of land. Money in Ireland has not accumulated into capital; industry has not risen to ambition; and, thence, while in England men climb from labor to aristocracy, in Ireland men descend from aristocracy to labor.

But the most grievous need of Ireland is the want of variety in occupation. Externally, Ireland is finely situated for commerce; internally, she is admirably constituted for manufactures. Commerce and manufactures would not only train the people to skill and independence, but relieve the soil from the pressure of an excessive population. The soil is the only source of life, and out of this fact come many evils; one of the worst is, that of extreme competition. Every vacant spot becomes an object of deadly strife. It is generally given to that person who offers the highest price, and shouts the loudest promise. He soon finds out in his despair, that he has undertaken too much. The landlord has spent no capital on it; the tenant has none to spend; and of the produce which is torn from its savage nakedness, the bulk goes to the absent proprietor and to the established church. The soil deteriorates ; the landlord will not lower his demands ; the tenant cannot pay them, and he is ejected. The landlord gives his place to another, and the ruined tenant knows not where to find a shelter. Though law has driven him out from his familiar hearth, nature compels him to return. He will prowl around the miserable abode that gave his poverty a refuge ; the hut that gave his little ones a home ; the roof that shielded the mother of his children. He cannot reason, his blood rushes back to its fountains, his whole nature is excited ; his brain is convulsed in delirium ; he is mad in his houseless distraction ; and in his madness, he slays, perhaps, his blameless successor. His former landlord is, possibly, a magistrate. This magistrate hands him to the constable ; the constable delivers him to the judge ; after due forms of trial, the judge consigns him to the executioner ; and the executioner closes the tragedy. This is but one of a hundred, that vary little in plot or incident. The scaffold is the stage, with which, as yet, Ireland has been the best acquainted ; and on that she has witnessed many a terrible drama, black, silent, bloody, and monstrous !

Who does not see in these circumstances, rudely as I have described them, the sources of enormous evils ? Passions, the deepest and most lasting, were kindled and kept burning by crushing men upon their own soil, by irritating them in those sentiments that all but the basest hold in reverence. Education was not only withheld, but punished; trade was not advanced, but restricted; home industry was suppressed, and foreign commerce was forbidden; and yet, men are now wondering that this work of folly and of guilt should still be felt. Why, it is not greatly over half a century, since any change for the better even began. But the effects of such a work does not pass away in fifty years.

What other effects, than those which we have seen, could be expected? Discontent, that outlives the provocation; anger, that survives the wrong; disorganization, that follows servitude and misrule; ignorance, deep and wide-spread, that bad legislation had long compelled, and that the best cannot hastily remove; idleness, that law made a habit or a necessity; poverty, coming out of idleness; crime and misery, issuing from both, a complication of entangled difficulties that shakes the hope of the philanthropist, and that baffles the wisdom of the statesman.

But the evils indicate their own remedies; and it is encouraging to see, in the progress of recent events, that national instincts are taking the direction that will gradually ameliorate national calamities. The Irish people must be respected; and they must be practically respected; they must have their due share in the legislation of the empire, and they must be fully represented, according to their numbers, their power, and their interests. There must grow up in Ireland, too, a social unity. Men of the same atmosphere must learn to love, and not to hate each other; they must join heart and hand, to promote the good of their common country; they must have hope for what is to come; they must have pardon for what is past. The law of tenure must be changed; the tenant must be protected. The landlord shall not be denied his rights; but he must be made to feel his duties. If he will not be true to his obligations, like all criminals, he ought to meet with punishment; and the punishment he can most feel, would be punishment on his purse. This, when written, was prophecy; much of it is now history; and the landlords have so contrived matters, as to prepare the punishment for themselves. Relieve the land of the horrible pressure that is on it; call in the amount of stalwart muscle that withers away in idleness, to healthy manufactures; let young men and maidens, that wander over earth for leave to toil, have but that liberty given them upon their own green island; and I shall challenge the world to show a happier or a handsomer race, men more generous, or women more lovely.

O, that all classes and all creeds would unite in a broad and generous sentiment of nationality; not a nationality of vanity and prejudice, but a nationality of brotherhood and peace. This would be for Ireland the day of her regeneration. To the eye, she is fair, indeed, among the nations; but to the heart, her beauty has been covered with sadness. Her fields are luxuriant, and her hills are green; yet the lot of her children has been in tears and blood. History, whose work at best is but melancholy, has written her story in despair. Hunger has lingered in her valleys; sickness in her dwellings; sin and madness in her secret places. Nature has given her a great largeness of bounty. Cattle cover her plains; the horn of plenty has been emptied on her vales; but sorrow and a curse have rained a blight on all. The airs of heaven blow upon her freshly; but they swell no sails, except those which are to bare her children into exile. The glorious sea girds her about; but it washes the shores of solitary harbors, and dashes an unloaded wave upon a virgin sand. A race of no mean capacities have lived in huts unworthy of the savage, and upon food almost too wretched for the brutes.

Ought it to be thus? Is this the design of nature? Is this the order of Providence? Is this a fatal and perpetual necessity? No, no, it is against the design of nature; it reverses the order of Providence; and the only necessity that belongs to it, is that which springs from misrule, mismanagement, and disunion. Let there be but a united people, and it cannot be longer thus; let divisions be abolished by a holy love of country, combined interests and combined activity will issue in general prosperity; let party names be lost in Irishman, and Irishman be a word for patriot; then, the sun of a new era will bathe with glory "the emerald set in the midst of the sea;" then, will the land of a common birth, be the land of a common heart; and then,

"Howe'er crowns and coronets be rent,
A virtuous populace will rise the while,
And stand, a wall of fire around their much-loved isle."

The course of these observations has led us along painful topics, but we will not leave them in despondency. If days which are gone, have left but painful memories, days that are to come may cheer us with bright and gracious hopes. If a soil the most fertile, has borne but a starving peasantry; if noble rivers have flowed unburdened to the sea; if capacious harbors have been ruffled by no freighted keels; if mines of wealth have slumbered untouched in the sleeping earth; still, I do not despair for my country. The soil is there yet in its beauty, and its children may yet live upon its fullness; the rivers are yet majestic, and will not always be a solitude; the broad and sheltered bay, that now mirrors but the mountains and the heavens, may yet reflect the snowy drapery of many a gallant ship; and the hills on which now the ragged and dejected shepherd wanders, may yet yield up their treasures to the light. Nature is not dead; nature is not dead in the works of creation or in the soul of man; nature is not dead, but ever in its generous beauty covers and supports us. No foolish passions can dry up the kindly heart of earth, or consume the fatness of the clouds, or shut out the glory of the skies. Nature yet survives; survives in her limitless bounty, survives in her eternal youth; and the people, though impoverished, are not destroyed. No wrongs have been able to crush them; no wars to render them inhuman. From every savage influence, they have come forth, not indeed uninjured, but yet not deeply degraded, nor ruthlessly depraved. From the worst experience in the history of nations, they have saved elements of excellence that may be shaped into the noblest civilization. From a long and dreary night of bondage, they have escaped with the vivid intellect, the cheerful temper, the affectionate spirit, the earnest, the hopeful enthusiasm that springs elastic from every sorrow.

The hour now seems dark in Ireland, but the light is

not quenched; it is only for a season obscured. The cloud is thick and broad; it rests heavily over the shivering millions; it is most dreary, and it seems filled with threatenings: but the moveless sun is shining tranquilly above it, in the benignant and the everlasting heavens. The cloud may break in tempest; but stillness and beauty will come when the hurricane has spent its strength, and the storm has passed away. But no tempest will, possibly, come at all. The cloud may dissolve in rain; it may give freshness, where it had only given gloom, and cool the ardor of the beams which it had excluded. Dark skies bring lightning; lightning brings the shower; then comes the sunshine on the grass, and all the fields are sparkling with glory and with gems.

Let me so think of the moral atmosphere that now hangs around and over Ireland. It is not to continue. God is in his universe, and guides the nations in their way. We will hold to our goodly trust, and in the strength of that earnest trust, we will firmly believe that He has rich blessings yet in store for Ireland. Where, often, we can see nothing but evil, our gracious Father is preparing good; and we will so believe it now, for sad, afflicted, mourning Ireland. O, land of my heart, of my fathers, and my birth! I will ever keep it in my thoughts, that God is looking down upon you with pity and with grace, and that He will call you up more brightly from your calamity. The times, indeed, seem bad, but suffering will leave its blessing. Plenty will come again; and humility, and gratitude, and mercy, and penitent and softened hearts will come along with it. Peace will be established; confidence will come with peace; capital will follow confidence; employment will increase with capital; education will be desired; knowledge will be diffused; and virtue will grow with knowledge. Yet, even if these things should not soon be; if all that is now anticipated, should long be hope deferred, and many a heart should sicken in waiting for relief; yet, I will not despond, I will not despond for Ireland; I will not despond for humanity; I will entertain no doubt in the agency which guides the world, and no mistrust in the destiny whereunto the world moves.

END OF VOL. I.

www.ingramcontent.com/pod-product-compliance
Lightning Source LLC
LaVergne TN
LVHW020242110826
845151LV00003B/1008
9781425528898